MW01068319

BUILDINGS
WITHOUT
ARCHITECTS
A GLOBAL GUIDE TO EVERYDAY ARCHITECTURE

John May

Anthony Reid, Consultant Editor

[handwritten inscription: 18/25/13 — To Fred Merry Christmas 2013 Love, Susan]

BUILDINGS WITHOUT ARCHITECTS

A GLOBAL GUIDE TO EVERYDAY ARCHITECTURE

RIZZOLI
NEW YORK

New York · Paris · London · Milan

First published in the United States of America in 2010
by Rizzoli International Publications, Inc.
300 Park Avenue South
New York, NY 10010
www.rizzoliusa.com

This book was conceived,
designed, and produced by
Ivy Press
210 High Street, Lewes
East Sussex BN7 2NS
www.ivy-group.co.uk

© 2010 Ivy Press Limited

All rights reserved. No part of this publication may be
reproduced, stored in a retrieval system, or transmitted
in any form or by any means, electronic, mechanical,
photocopying, recording, or otherwise, without prior
consent of the publishers.

2010 2011 2012 2013 / 10 9 8 7 6 5 4 3 2 1

ISBN: 978-0-8478-3361-0

Library of Congress Control Number: 2009936367

CREATIVE DIRECTOR Peter Bridgewater
PUBLISHER Jason Hook
CONCEIVED BY Sophie Collins
EDITORIAL DIRECTOR Caroline Earle
ART DIRECTOR Michael Whitehead
DESIGNER Martin Topping
ILLUSTRATOR Coral Mula
PICTURE MANAGER Katie Greenwood

Printed and bound in China

CONTENTS

FOREWORD
ANTHONY REID

We humans have an amazing ability to innovate. Nowhere is this more apparent than in the world's diverse range of handmade or vernacular buildings. In the pages of this book, John May has carefully detailed key examples from around the world of this highly important, yet little-known building form.

Vernacular architecture is a subject that provides a window on the lives and traditions of the indigenous people of our world, and in so doing creates a mirror that reflects our own experiences. This, in turn, helps us to understand more clearly where the buildings of our contemporary world spring from, and, more importantly, why such buildings so often fail to meet our fundamental human needs.

It takes little imagination to appreciate the disastrous long-term effects that, for example, high-density, high-rise housing has had on the communities and social cohesion of our world's cities. The notion that houses should be "machines for living" long resonated in the mind-set of many planners and architects. Education systems provided an aesthetic awareness and certain expertise. Rationally applied building technology and forms matched the required "function" of the building. Solutions were fixed, immovable, and sold as a modern utopian ideal to the world's aspiring urban classes.

However, if we look at both current and historical vernacular building traditions, there exist opportunities to learn of solutions to our housing needs that draw less on the limited resources available to us. These impact more gently on our fragile ecosystems, offering solutions that engender a profound connection between the builders, their environment, the materials used, and the wider community.

Much has been written, and indeed understood, about human-scale architecture and the need to limit the environmental impact of the building industry. However, the truly sustainable practitioners are still widely ignored by the majority of the establishment, where the champions and practitioners of vernacular building are still marginalized, either through misinformed opinion or by the forces of property speculation and planning policy.

It may be that the notion of tradition leaves people feeling un-easy, with associations to a world of convention and constraint; they feel that traditions belong to a place in the past, inhabited by the ghosts of disapproving ancestors. However, tradition can also be our guide and teacher, and provide the template for architectural solutions that can stretch the imagination far beyond the seemingly

This renovated "Black House" in the Outer Hebrides symbolizes the enduring nature of vernacular architecture. The form of these low-lying, stone-built, thatched longhouses is perfectly suited to the harsh, windswept Scottish landscape.

rational. In a world where the politicians and the policy makers are struggling to find effective solutions to the problems that threaten the very existence of our world, it is time for individuals to take the initiative and look seriously at the creativity inherent in the vernacular buildings of our world.

As the author describes in the introduction, this book is a global journey. I would add that this is a journey that will ultimately lead us all back home, and in so doing, it reveals new perspectives and insights into this very special place where we make our lives.

GALLERY OF BUILDING MEDIA

Vernacular architecture, by its very nature, is built from local materials that are readily on hand and is thus defined by the geology and ecology of the region, as well as by local climatic conditions. Constructed by the community using traditional tools, these structures are highly practical, energy efficient, and blend with the landscape. These buildings carry many of the attributes that we are now seeking in "green architecture" as we struggle to adapt our built environment to the demands and concerns of the climate-change era.

WOOD

The immense forests of the northern and southern hemispheres have traditionally provided a ready source of construction material for many kinds of vernacular buildings. The structural properties of wood, its strength and length, make it ideal for the framework of a building, and also for walls, floors, and roofs.

ABOVE The striking gable end of a wood-frame Hallenhaus house barn, many of which still survive in the eastern Netherlands and northern Germany. The building is supported by a post-and-truss system of wood beams.

RIGHT Giant cruck frames—made from two halves of a single tree, joined together so their curves mirror each other—provide the main structural support for this thirteenth-century tithe barn, located near Bath, England.

ABOVE The distinctive three-tier structure of a Carpathian Lemko church, built entirely of intersecting wood logs with wood shingle roofs topped by spires and cupolas.

LEFT This Slovenian hayrack, known as a *kozolec*, is a simple wood, freestanding structure with a small thatched or wood shingle roof for shelter. The four main posts provide support for the racks, which are themselves made of thin wood poles.

ABOVE These Japanese *minka* ("houses of the people") are built in the *gasshō-zukuri* (steep-slope roof) style, the thatched roofs being designed to shrug off the heavy snows of winter. Their sturdy wood frames and internal bamboo screens are appropriate technologies for earthquake regions.

RIGHT A fine example of an urban minka *(machiya)*, a long narrow row house fronted with wood grilles, and supported by a framework of wood columns, beams, and braces.

RIGHT These beautiful hand-crafted wood houses—built by the Zafimaniry people of southeast Madagascar—have walls formed of vertical planking, wood roofs, and ornamental window shutters, all assembled using wood pegs and mortise-and-tenon joints.

ABOVE The simple two-room Caribbean chattel house was originally built entirely of wood, without using nails, so that it could be readily disassembled and moved from place to place.

LEFT A strikingly carved totem pole stands guard in front of the highly decorated facade of a Haida house on the Queen Charlotte Islands, off British Columbia, Canada. Such houses have two to eight wood beams forming their main framework, with wood plank walls and wood roofs.

RIGHT This unusual twelve-sided barn near Pullman, Washington, is built entirely of wood with a giant wood shingle roof and two large dormer windows on opposite ends.

ABOVE This shows the typical style of wood church building on the island of Chiloé off the coast of Chile, with its rectangular basilica divided into three naves by wood columns, a roofed portico, a main roof of wood shingles, and a symmetrical tower at one end.

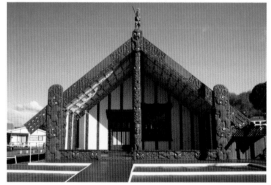

LEFT The imposing façade of a Maori meetinghouse, with its carved barge boards and post, fronts a large rectangular building supported by a wood post-and-beam structure, with walls of wood clapboards and a corrugated iron roof.

LEFT A view of two of the many thatched wood pavilions that sit within a walled compound and which together form a traditional Bali house *(kuren)*.

RIGHT A large traditional hollow-post drainage mill near Cabouw in the Netherlands, which was used to draw water from the land. The thatched, wood-base structure provided a home for the miller and his family.

ABOVE An elegant and sizable example of a Russian *izba*, a wood house with a small attached barn, built of logs with interlocking corners and a sloping wood shingle roof. The posts of the wood portico, eaves, window frames, and doors are carved and embellished (see detail left).

LEFT This is an example of a common northern form of izba, the two-story *koshel* (basket house) in which the living quarters and the agricultural spaces are integrated into one building.

ABOVE A simple one-room log cabin provided a basic rudimentary dwelling for many pioneer settlers in North America. Overlapping corner notches help fit the logs more securely and tightly together. The stone chimney is a later addition.

RIGHT An elegant wood building built by one of the Shaker communities in the United States. It demonstrates their basic approach to architecture and design, which emphasizes simplicity and utility.

STONE

The earliest dwellings were cave shelters carved out of stone and rocks; many in the Mediterranean are still occupied. Other ancient forms of building were dwellings with dry-stone walls or roofs, built without mortar. In India, elaborate step wells and stepped ponds are a testament to the skills of the stonemasons of the past.

LEFT, ABOVE, AND RIGHT Three views of the extraordinary cave houses of Cappadocia, a region of Anatolia, central Turkey. A landscape composed of soft tufa, it has been carved by the wind and weather into strange shapes that were then occupied by early Christian settlers who constructed large underground towns and settlements. Above ground, the most distinctive features of the landscape are the so-called fairy chimneys (left), which have, for centuries, been turned into multistoried dwellings with rooms, staircases, and windows hand-carved out of the soft volcanic rock. Many of these are still occupied, and the whole area has become a major tourist destination.

ABOVE A stunning view of the extraordinary network of cave houses that make up the *Sassi* of Matera, in southern Italy. The houses stretch deep into the rock and have been continually occupied for centuries.

RIGHT A Spanish cave house to which external buildings have been attached. This is a common feature in Andalusia, where many cave dwellings have been renovated on ancient sites and are now reoccupied.

ABOVE Found mainly in the desert states of Gujarat and Rajasthan in India, these ancient Indian step wells, designed to store the monsoon rains, are amazing examples of stone craftsmanship and engineering.

RIGHT The strange and wonderful stepped ponds of India, with their zigzag stairs, were constructed near temples and used for bathing and rituals. Built of stone blocks, each flight of stairs is a matched pair placed side-by-side.

ABOVE A side view of a Hebridean Black House, showing the exterior dry-stone wall and thatched roof. In fact, the building is ringed by two thick dry-stone walls running in parallel with a gap in between, forming a rectangle with rounded corners.

LEFT, BELOW, AND RIGHT Three views of the stone houses, or *trulli*, in the Apulia region of southeast Italy, which have double dry-stone walls (below left) built of local stone and conical roofs made of overlapping limestone slabs. The biggest concentration of these houses is found in the town of Alberobello and typically comprises rectangular buildings containing several square rooms connected by semicircular arches. The pointed ogival roofs are topped with a plastered "hat" culminating in a pinnacle. As can be seen in the two main photographs, the unpainted roofs are often decorated with mythological and religious symbols of various kinds.

EARTH AND CLAY

One half of the world's population—approximately three billion people—live or work in buildings created of earth, mud, or clay. They are found on all continents and vary in shape and size from individual shelters, such as a Mousgoum *tolek,* to vast ceremonial buildings, such as the Great Mosque at Djenné.

ABOVE This pretty pink thatched house in the English county of Devon has thick walls built of cob, a building material made by mixing fiber and water with clay and aggregate.

LEFT An overhead view of one of the desert towns of Iran that are built entirely of adobe bricks. The distinctive towers of the wind catchers provide a flow of air through the buildings.

RIGHT The facade of a row of well-established Chinese *yao dong,* man-made earth-sheltered family dwellings that are dug into the side of a cliff. They face south to gain the maximum sunlight.

LEFT The distinctive form of a Mousgoum *tolek*, glimpsed through the brightly painted compound entrance. Toleks are handcrafted out of layered balls of clay. The protruding ribs add solidity and provide footholds to aid construction without the use of scaffolding.

RIGHT The extraordinary earthen roundhouse of the Batammaliba people of Benin and Togo is one of the great examples of African vernacular architecture. The thatched towers are granaries that flank the main opening.

RIGHT AND BELOW The imposing buttresses and protective walls of the Great Mosque of Djenné, in Mali, form the largest mud-brick building in the world. They are punctuated with ceramic pipes, to direct water away from the walls, and palm branches that help to reduce cracking and also serve as ready-made scaffolding for the annual repairs. These are carried out at a spring festival in which the entire community takes part.

ABOVE The painted mud and thatch houses of the Ndebele people have gained worldwide attention due to the striking nature of their exterior artwork, which is painted entirely by the women of the tribe.

LEFT A partial view of the adobe walls of the Taos Pueblo in northern New Mexico, which was originally built between AD 1000 and 1450 and has been continually occupied ever since. The roof of each level is supported by beams of pine.

RIGHT These remarkable tower houses in Yemen are built of sun-dried clay, mud blocks, or fired bricks on a stone foundation. Originating as defensive towers, they are an ideal structure for housing an extended family.

POLES, POSTS, AND COVERINGS

These varied shelters from many parts of the world use flexible poles of various kinds to create a basic framework, which is then covered with thatching. Such a construction method is also used by nomadic peoples to create lightweight shelters that can easily be erected and disassembled.

LEFT An aerial view of a Yanomami *shabano* in the Amazon forests of southern Venezuela. This communal structure has a framework of hardwood poles covered with a canopy of slender saplings thatched with palm leaves.

BELOW One of the stilt houses of the town of Ganvié on Lake Nikoué in Benin. The house is supported on mangrove poles, which are also used as a framework for the wattle walls and the hipped roof, thatched with grass.

ABOVE The framework of the Zulu *indlu* consists of a ring of saplings that cross each other at right angles. The roof is supported by posts and beams, and the whole structure is thatched with grass, secured by a net of grass ropes.

LEFT The distinctive four-sided thatched roofs of the Tzotzils' *chukal na* in the Mexican state of Chiapas. This rectangular single-room house has a framework made of oak or cypress posts topped with wood beams that support a pyramid of rafters and posts, covered with a wattle structure and thatch.

RIGHT A Korowai tree house in the remote rain forests of West Papua, Indonesia, built around a tree and supported by a network of wood poles secured firmly in the ground. The house has a floor of wood spars, wattle walls, and a thatched roof.

BELOW This *fale tele,* a type of roundhouse, is a building unique to the islands of Samoa. The structure is entirely supported in the center by three wood posts, which hold up a matted covering made of coconut or sugar cane, thatched with fronds and leaves. This rests on an outer ring of posts.

ABOVE The distinctive *tipi* of the native Americans is made up of four elements—a set of wood poles that form the basic structure, a semicircular covering of skin or canvas, an inner lining, and a door flap.

ABOVE RIGHT The Mongolian *ger* is built from a ring of expandable lattice panels of flexible willow, which support a roof framework of bent poles. The tent is covered with felt mats fastened by ropes woven from animal hair.

CENTER RIGHT The *min*, the nomadic home of the Rendille camel nomads of northern Kenya, consists of a whelk-shape structure made of wood poles covered with overlapping tiles made of sisal.

RIGHT Various forms of the black tent are used by nomadic groups across a huge arc from Mauritania, in west Africa, to Tibet, in east Asia. The tent's main structure is formed by a varying arrangement of poles, secured by ropes and pegs, with a covering of goat hair.

BAMBOO

Bamboo, which is native to five continents, has been used as a structural material in vernacular buildings for two millennia. It has a high strength-to-weight ratio and can be worked with simple tools. Fast-growing and easily harvested, bamboo looks set to provide a valuable sustainable building resource for the future.

RIGHT The dramatic shape of the *korambos* ("spirit houses") of the Abelam people of New Guinea dominates the village. They are built of a framework of bamboo rafters and poles, fastened to a sloping ridge pole and covered with thatch.

RIGHT These *paisa* houses, common in the mountainous coffee-growing region of Colombia, are built almost entirely of bamboo, which is surprisingly earthquake resistant. The roof spaces are used for drying coffee beans.

ABOVE The huge extended boat-shape saddleback roofs of the *tongkonan,* the ancestral houses of the Toraja people of central Sulawesi, sit on a wood cabin supported by thick wood posts. The thatched roof is built of bamboo poles overlaid with layers of bamboo staves.

LEFT The curved roof of the beautiful half-barrel-shape huts of the Toda people of southern India consists of bundles of thin bamboo bent over bamboo poles; this is overlain by a dense covering of thin bamboo canes running horizontally and topped by a thick thatch of swamp grass.

REED

Reed is widely used for thatching and to produce woven mats for cladding, but less commonly for structural purposes. The two best-known examples of reed builders are the distinctive communities of the Marsh Arabs of Iraq and the Urus people of Lake Titicaca.

ABOVE The impressive cathedral-like *mudhifs,* built by the Marsh Arabs of Iraq, are the largest reed buildings in the world. Large arches of reed bundles are strengthened at the top and sides by additional long reed bundles.

RIGHT A reed builder cuts off the top of a reed bundle, used to support the mudhif walls.

LEFT A traditional rectangular Urus reed house is flanked by two tipi-type reed structures, built on a floating island of reeds.

RECYCLED MATERIALS

The use of scrap and waste materials as a building resource is one of the most important trends in modern vernacular architecture. In the squatter cities of the developing world, vast areas of ad hoc buildings provide shelter to poor rural immigrants. In the West, increasing use of discarded materials is driven by new imperatives to create low-energy, low-carbon buildings.

ABOVE A giant squatter settlement on the edge of Caracas, Venezuela's capital and largest city, stretches up the hillside. Squatter cities are spreading across the world and increasing in both size and number. Here, homes are made from whichever materials come on hand, and temporary structures gradually evolve into permanent dwellings.

RIGHT Earthships are passive solar homes made out of recycled and natural materials. The thick walls of the building, which can be designed in many shapes and forms, are composed of recycled car tires packed with earth. Much use is also made of recycled cans and bottles.

LEFT The Wat Pa Maha Chedi Kaew temple in Thailand was constructed using one million beer bottles that were collected by Buddhist monks.

SNOW

One of the most iconic of all vernacular buildings, the Inuit igloo is both ingenious and simple, a snow-block dome built without the use of any supporting structure. Constructed in a wide variety of sizes, the best-known is the smallest, which is used as a temporary shelter for hunters and can be built in a matter of hours.

ABOVE A sturdy igloo with a long sunken entrance tunnel, which acts as a cold sink and helps to maintain warmth within the igloo. Loose snow is used to cover the snow-blocks and seal the cracks between them to provide extra insulation.

LEFT A view of the igloo during construction, showing how the snow blocks are arranged in a spiral, with each additional layer leaning inward to create the domed shape.

INTRODUCTION
JOHN MAY

This book is an introductory guide to, and a global tour of, some of the world's vernacular architecture, which is most simply defined as the architecture of the people, designed and built by communities, families, and individual builders. It is also a book with a message: vernacular architecture is an important global issue for our time.

The authority on this vast subject is Paul Oliver, who initiated and edited the standard publication on the subject, the massive three-volume *Encyclopedia of Vernacular Architecture* (impossible to buy but available in some libraries), and many other key works, including *Dwellings*. The definition he uses in both the encyclopedia and *Dwellings* to define his subject is: "the dwellings and all other buildings of the people. Related to their environmental contexts and available resources, they are owner- or community-built, utilizing traditional technologies. All forms of vernacular architecture are built to meet specific needs, accommodating the values, economies, and ways of life of the cultures that produced them." To which could be added, "They may be adapted or developed over time as needs and circumstances change."

In another of Paul Oliver's works, *Atlas of Vernacular Architecture of the World*, produced with his colleague Marcel Velinga, we learn some extraordinary things. Among them, that "no one knows exactly, or even approximately, how many buildings there are in the world, but estimates of well over a billion have been made." Of these, eighty percent or more are estimated to be vernacular buildings. Put another way, buildings designed and built by professional architects and builders constitute only a small part of the world's built infrastructure. The vast majority of people in the world live in homes and use buildings that they and their friends and family have built themselves.

This is obviously more true in some countries and regions than in others. In the Western world, planning restrictions limit self-building, land is expensive, and the traditions of our forebears and ancestors have been marginalized, their skills lost and forgotten. In other large parts of the world—in Africa, Asia, and Latin America—people are closer to their vernacular architecture, and in many cases are still living in it and building it. However, the situation is changing fast. The rush to modernization means that more people than ever before are moving to cities, where vast numbers now live in squatter settlements where they construct houses from waste and scrap. This is the new vernacular architecture of our time.

This impressive fortlike structure is a circular *tulou* in the Fujian province of southwest China, a communal dwelling originally built to protect the inhabitants from armed bandits. A group of forty-six of these remarkable buildings are now included on UNESCO's World Heritage List, but vernacular architecture in China is generally under threat.

All over the world, meanwhile, traditional vernacular architecture is disappearing—not only the building forms themselves, but also the knowledge, skills, and customs behind their creation. China is an outstanding example of the battle being fought to protect vernacular building forms from the march of the bulldozers. Academics and NGOs are seeking to educate the country's policy makers about the value and importance of preserving traditional architecture, but their efforts are outweighed by the huge commercial pressures driving a rush to modernization. And now we come to another world issue: how are we going to house our new arrivals? As of August 3, 2009, the earth's population is estimated by the United States Census Bureau to be 6.775 billion; it is expected to reach 9 billion by 2040. We are not going to be able to house our future generations in concrete blocks. Apart from other considerations, climate-change predictions and concern over the rise in atmospheric carbon dioxide precludes this. For each new bag of cement, a bag and a half of carbon dioxide is created as waste. This is why many architects and designers, aid organizations, and others are looking at vernacular architecture to learn how to build using local materials and live lightly on the earth.

Any examination of vernacular building is full of surprises and, by its very nature, interdisciplinary. These buildings do not exist in a vacuum—they are built as part of people's lives and culture. These structures are shaped not only by physical circumstances and available materials, but also by the beliefs, myths, customs, and traditions of the tribe, clan, or group that builds them. Early vernacular shelters were once considered "primitive," whereas now we look on them with more respect, noting the ingenuity employed to fashion functional and aesthetically pleasing structures with simple tools.

It is fascinating to consider the wide variety of structures in which people choose to live, which includes tents and caves, pile dwellings, courtyard houses, log cabins, and mud towers. Also noteworthy is the manner in which similar basic materials—such as earth, brick, stone, wood, bamboo, palm, and reed—can be employed for different purposes. Forms are expressed in whatever material is close on hand. Therefore, a roof may be made out of almost anything: grass thatch, clay tiles, wood shingles, or corrugated iron.

The majority of examples given in this book are houses, but we have also investigated the step wells of India, the churches of Chile, the windmills of Holland, the big barns of the United States, and the bee houses of Slovenia, which remind us that vernacular building is a broad term, including places of work and worship and communal facilities. Many vernacular buildings are beautiful as well as functional. Some demonstrate a wealth of detail and decoration. Doors and windows are carved with geometric motifs, walls are elaborately painted, and domes are topped with ostrich eggs and finials.

Above all, vernacular design must be practical. Nomadic peoples build lightweight structures that can easily be packed up and reassembled; sedentary peoples build permanent homes that can last five hundred years, during which time they are constantly renewed and adapted to suit changing requirements. As a general rule, vernacular builders aim to stay warm in winter and cool in summer, and they have devised numerous ingenious techniques for achieving those ends. The desert architecture of Iran incorporated air-conditioning systems that have a great deal to teach today's house builders, who must tackle the uncertainties of climate change.

A traditional wood shack in Georgia. Wood cabins and shacks of all shapes, sizes, and styles are a vernacular feature across huge areas of the great American landscape.

Many vernacular buildings around the world are devoted to revered ancestors. These buildings are often constructed in precise alignments according to spiritual beliefs. The interiors are arranged in a similar manner, with precisely placed central hearths and shrines to the family. In Madagascar (see the Zafimaniry House, pages 114–15), the family home coevolves with the relationship of the couple who live in it. In other examples that we have selected, the women are in sole charge of house building, or their role may be to paint and decorate. In almost all cases of vernacular building, women and men inhabit separate, clearly defined spaces.

Such is the wide variety of vernacular forms, which encompasses towers and domes, subterranean dwellings, giant circular communal fortresses, meetinghouses, cabins, shacks, and huts, that this collection is inevitably partial and selective. We have covered the globe, drawing interesting examples from each region, and have tried to profile a satisfying mixture of structures in order to do justice to the subject's complexity. We hope you enjoy the global journey and that some of our enthusiasm rubs off on you. You may even be inspired to build your own handmade house.

Dense living conditions, past and present: The cave houses of Matera in southern Italy (below left), whose built facades lead into a cave dwelling behind; the modern squatter city of Dharavi in Mumbai (below right), India, where some one million people live in makeshift houses constructed of scrap and recycled materials. Such dwellings are the most common vernacular buildings of our time.

FROM DUTCH WINDMILLS
TO GERMAN BARNS

Our journey across Europe and Eurasia commences in the far north with the different forms of shelter used by the Sami people. We highlight two forms of earth buildings, found at the extreme ends of their territory, and the cruck wood frame, of which Britain has the greatest density in the world. We profile the giant housebarns of northern Germany and the unique wood churches of the Ukraine, as well as the many forms of izba found across vast swathes of Russia. In addition, we admire the working windmills of the Netherlands and the practical and elegant hayracks and bee houses of Slovenia.

SAMI GAMME AND GOATTE

The Sami are an indigenous people, scattered across the northern territories of Norway, Sweden, Finland, and Russia. Some groups of Sami lived a semi-settled life on the coast and in the fjords, supplementing their farming with wild game and fish from the forest and the sea. The pastoral nomadic Sami were principally reindeer herders who, to this day, follow the animals through the winter and spend the summer by the coast.

The coastal Sami built turfed winter dwellings of various kinds called *gahti* or *gamme* (pl. *gammer*), all of which were based on a skeleton frame of wood rafters covered with turf. The oldest kind was round at its base and had a domelike form. The semi-settled coastal Sami built larger, more solid turf huts. Some groups of Sami, who became permanently settled and took up dairy farming, developed larger versions—the rectangular "joint gamme" building—in which people and livestock shared the same house. In the twentieth century, many Sami moved into small two-room wood houses, with adjoining farm buildings made of turf or logs.

The Sami began building a gamme by constructing two arches from birch wood. The arches were then linked by a birch pole at the top and another that ran along the side of the arch. A well-built gamme could last thirty years or more.

The nomadic Sami of Northern Norway use a transportable tent dwelling called a *goatte,* which employs a similar type of arched wood frame as the turf houses, covered by canvas in the summer and a double layer of woollen rugs during the winter.

The Sami peoples protected their food supplies from marauding animals, such as wolverines, by building storehouses. These were huts, solidly constructed of horizontal logs, notched at the corners; the whole was raised off the ground either on four corner poles (to make an *aite*) or on one or two tree trunks with roots *(njalla)*.

SEE ALSO
> Mongolian Ger, pages 94–95

> Rendille Min, pages 112–13

> Plains Indian Tipi, pages 126–27

MATERIALS
* Lumber for wood framework: two arches linked by long pole

* Turf for outer covering

* Reindeer skin and roundwood for nomadic shelters

Sami is the name of the cultural region traditionally inhabited by the Sami people, which covers an area of about 150,000 square miles (388,350 sq km).

NORTHERN SCANDINAVIA/ RUSSIA

EARLY GAMME

This is the oldest form of Sami dwelling, constructed of bow-shaped rafters and vertical poles, covered first with birch bark and then with a layer of turf. These were used not only for living accommodation, but also as storehouses, animal shelters, or as huts.

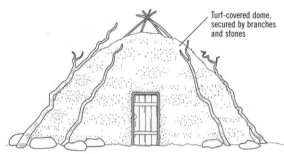

Turf-covered dome, secured by branches and stones

RECTANGULAR GAMME

The interiors of both the dome-shape and rectangular forms of the gamme are constructed in a similar manner. For a rectangular gamme, two parallel rows of poles are arranged vertically from floor to ceiling, creating a narrow corridor running from the door to the back wall. The hearth is placed in the center, with a smoke hole above and a kitchen behind it.

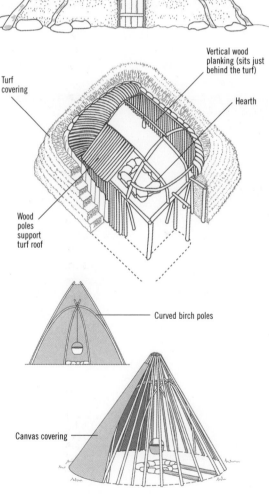

Vertical wood planking (sits just behind the turf)

Turf covering

Hearth

Wood poles support turf roof

GOATTE

The main supports of the nomadic Sami's "bent-pole" tent are two pairs of curved birch poles to which numerous side poles are attached to support the fabric of the canvas wall. All these poles are light, making them easy to handle and transport. The tent takes about thirty minutes to erect or dismantle.

Curved birch poles

Canvas covering

FROM DUTCH WINDMILLS TO GERMAN BARNS
HEBRIDEAN BLACK HOUSE

Once common in the islands and highlands of Scotland, mainly built in the mid-nineteenth century, and evolved from an older form, Black Houses (*taigh dubh* in Gaelic) survive, and are still in use, only on the Hebridean islands. Perfectly suited to the harsh local climate, these single-story thatched longhouses, low-lying and rounded with thick walls, present little resistance to the prevailing winds sweeping in from the Atlantic. Their name may have come from the fact that, without a chimney, these houses soon acquired a blackened interior.

The construction of a Black House began with the building of two dry-stone walls—as broad as they were high (up to 6½ feet/ 2 m thick), tapering toward the top—that ran in parallel, with a gap in between, forming a rectangle with rounded corners.

The gap was filled with pebbles, rubble, and sand overlain with turf, and formed a grass-covered "path," which sheep would climb up and graze on. These strong, durable walls ensured the houses were well insulated, and also soundproofed them against the constant howl of wind and the crash of the ocean.

Because there are no trees on the Hebridean islands, the components that supported the thatch roof were mainly driftwood that had been washed ashore, often carried by the Gulf Stream from North America or the Caribbean. These were laid across the inside wall and topped by a thatch of two layers of turf overlain with cereal straw, which was then draped with old fishing nets, tied down with heather ropes, and weighted by large stones.

According to Donald John Maclennan, who was born in one, "because of the shortage of wood, and the toil involved in collecting stone, families often built houses back-to-back, sharing a common wall." Inside the Black House, a family would live at one end, and animals (mainly cattle) at the other. Traditional Black Houses were still lived in as late as the 1970s.

SEE ALSO

> Zulu Indlu, pages 116–17

> Ndebele Painted House, pages 118–19

MATERIALS

* Stone for two walls, infilled with pebbles, rubble, and sand

* Driftwood for roof supports

* Turf and cereal straw for thatch, tied down with heather ropes

The Inner and Outer Hebridean Islands form an archipelago off the west coast of Scotland.

HEBRIDEAN
ISLANDS,
SCOTLAND

CROSS SECTION

This cross section of a Black House, viewed from the wood gable end, shows clearly the two stone walls running in parallel with a gap in between, the hearth in the center, and the heather ropes, weighted by stones, used to secure the thatch; this was renewed annually, the old smoky thatch making excellent fertilizer.

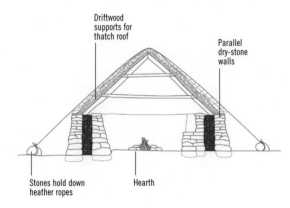

Driftwood supports for thatch roof

Parallel dry-stone walls

Stones hold down heather ropes

Hearth

TRADITIONAL BLACK HOUSE

This shows the solidity of the low-lying thatched longhouse. Inside a Black House, a family would live at one end, animals (mainly cattle) at the other. An open-hearth fire burned dried peat and gave off smoky fumes. The people would often sleep in recesses in the thickness of the wall behind the fireplace.

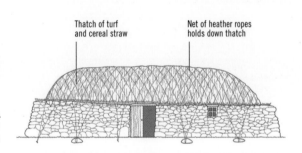

Thatch of turf and cereal straw

Net of heather ropes holds down thatch

MODERN BLACK HOUSE

This first modern version of a Black House was built in four months in 1993, in the traditional way using local materials, but with the addition of windows, a chimney, and modern conveniences, such as a toilet. It serves as a guesthouse for tourists.

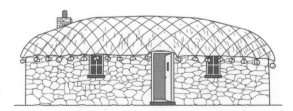

CRUCK-FRAME BUILDINGS

The origin of cruck-frame buildings is open to speculation, because there is little evidence of examples before 1200. They are preeminently found in Britain, where four thousand have been recorded, mainly in the north and in the west of the country, with none in the eastern and southeastern lowland. Crucks are also found, in fewer numbers, in many areas of France, in Northern Ireland, and Scandinavia.

Building a cruck frame involved the use of an entire tree trunk or the main branch of a large tree, which was split down the middle, the two halves (known as "blades") being positioned in an A-frame shape so that the curve on each mirrors the other, and fastened at the top by a "collar" or tie beam. A series of these, erected at intervals, would be linked together by a ridge board and by two side rails at the level of the eaves. Smaller pieces were arranged in triangles within the framework to act as wind braces. The roof was formed of rafters, running from ridge to side rail, which carried the thatch.

Because the framing supported the weight of the roof, the walls were only required to keep out the weather and were made variously of wattle and daub, turf, clay, and—from the sixteenth century onward—stone. To help minimize rot, the feet of a cruck frame were commonly stood on rounded padstones.

By the end of the Middle Ages, there was a critical shortage of large trees, so Henry VIII tried to stop cruck construction in order to save the trees that were left for use by the Navy. As a result, box framing, an alternative method that used smaller lumber components yet less lumber overall, and was already dominant in the east and southeast of England, began to spread across the rest of the country.

Box framing became popular for residential buildings because it enabled the building of second and third floors, and also made it easier to add extra wings to a building.

SEE ALSO

> Natural Building, pages 180–81

> Big Barn, pages 128–29

MATERIALS

* Tree trunk or large branch, split into two, fastened with a tie beam. Also wood for frame components

* Wattle and daub, turf, clay, or stone for walls

* Thatch for roof

The biggest concentration of cruck frames is in Britain; they are also scattered in areas of France and Scandinavia.

UK/FRANCE/
SCANDINAVIA

THE CRUCK FRAME

The completed cruck frame is made up of three crucks linked together by a ridge board and by two side rails. In medieval times, the timber for the crucks would have been felled with a two-man saw and ax, squared up with an adze (an axlike tool with an arched blade used for shaping wood), assembled on the ground, and then raised.

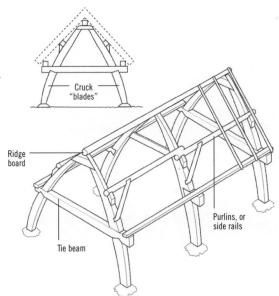

Cruck "blades"

Ridge board

Purlins, or side rails

Tie beam

CRUCK-FRAME HOUSE

This cutaway diagram of a cruck-frame house shows clearly the full extent of the additional wood framing added to the initial structure, including the rafters with thatch topping. Since *c.* 1980 in the UK, there has been a revival in new buildings using green oak and incorporating cruck frames.

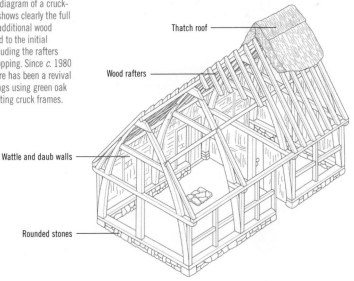

Thatch roof

Wood rafters

Wattle and daub walls

Rounded stones

COB HOUSE

Cob is an earth-base building material comprising subsoil, clay, sand, and gravel, which is mixed with straw and water to a stiff but malleable mass and used to build the walls of a house and numerous items within it, including shelves, benches, floors, and ovens.

People have likely been building cob houses of various kinds since prehistoric times, and such houses and shelters can be found in many parts of the world, including the United States, parts of Europe, and Africa, as well as Australia and New Zealand.

Exactly when cob building originated in England is not known, but it has certainly been in use since the fifteenth century and was one of the primary methods of building construction for all social classes up until the early 1800s, when fired bricks became readily available. The oldest surviving cob structures in the UK are seven hundred years old, and there are approximately fifty thousand cob buildings still in use in England today. One of the main centers of cob building is the southwest of England, particularly Devon; the word *cob* is an old Devon word for a mud wall. Devon is one of the wetter counties in England, so the mixture of ingredients in the cob—which includes a naturally occurring aggregate called shillet—is constituted for a wet climate.

Cob building has many advantages: the cob walls, when dry, are extremely hard and will last for centuries; they can be shaped to any required form using a sharp spade or mattock; cob is load-bearing, so cob houses need no wood framework. The only disadvantage is that because the building process involves various stages, the total construction time may be as much as fifteen months.

Cob walls are commonly rendered with permeable lime-base coatings and paint to enable the walls to breathe and moisture to evaporate. Most cob houses are thatched, with overhanging eaves.

SEE ALSO

> Vernacular Revivals, pages 182–83

> Ndebele Painted House, pages 118–19

MATERIALS

* Stone foundations
* Subsoil, clay, sand, and gravel, mixed with straw and water, for cob walls
* Lime-base coating to enable walls to breathe
* Thatch for roof

Devon has a tradition of cob houses, built of local materials to suit the wet climate.

SOUTHWEST ENGLAND

COB HOUSE

This is a grand and conventional style of cob house, but cob houses come in many shapes, sizes, and styles. The thickness of the cob-house walls—the average in a Devon cob is 2 feet (60 cm)—means they are warm in winter and cool in summer.

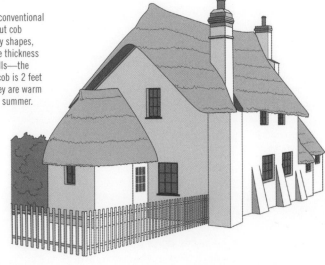

FOUNDATIONS

Building with cob is a slow and very labor-intensive process. The cob is mixed using hands and feet or, for larger projects, a cement mixer or power machinery. It is then loaded onto stone foundations, which prevent damp. Each layer, or "lift"— typically 2 feet (60 cm) high and 2–3 feet (60–90 cm) thick—is shaped by hand and trodden down to compress it.

Stone foundations

First "lift" of cob— earth, clay, sand, and gravel mixed with straw and water

LIFTS

Each lift needs several days to dry out before the next is added. As a result, it can take three months or more to make a two-story building. It can then take six to nine months for the thick walls to dry out completely, in the process of which they will shrink. Only after this has happened can doors and deep-set windows be added.

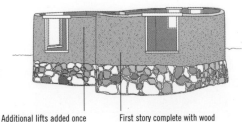

Additional lifts added once each has dried, until the building is complete

First story complete with wood window frames in place

HALLENHAUS HOUSE BARN

Once found in a wide arc right across the eastern Netherlands and north Germany, the *Hallenhaus* (pl. *Hallenhäuser*/Hall-House) is a form of wood-frame house barn that contained, under one roof, living quarters, stables, and crop store. It was in use from the fifteenth to the twentieth centuries and numerous fine examples survive to this day. The basic three-aisle form of the Hallenhaus possibly developed from an early longhouse of the seventh to tenth centuries, to which the aisles were gradually added. Although there is a great deal of regional styling and variation in construction details, the basic form of the Hallenhaus remained consistent throughout.

The support system for the central nave of the building was constructed in a post-and-truss form, with long beams running across the top of parallel rows of posts, capped with a wood framework. This wide hall space *(Diele),* which was covered with large floorboards, was used for all important tasks, including the threshing in wintertime. On either side of the Diele were the stables and stalls, for cattle and horses. Hallenhäuser can be categorized by the number of animal bays they have—the smallest would have two, the largest ten or more, stretching for up to 148 feet (45 m) in length. At the far end of the Diele was a living and sleeping area for the farmer, his family, and farmworkers, arranged around a central open hearth.

The large, steep roof was thatched and the exterior walls were wood frames with panels in between made of wattle and daub or bricks. Many examples of Hallenhäuser have an older interior framework, as the outer walls and rafters, which are not integral to the main structure, have been replaced at some point in the building's history. The entrance to the larger form of Hallenhaus was big enough to accommodate a horse and wagon; at harvest times, the corn was loaded up into the empty space above the Diele.

SEE ALSO

> Big Barn,
  pages 128–29

> Japanese Minka,
  pages 86–87

MATERIALS

* Lumber for wood
  frame post-and-
  truss system

* Wattle and daub or
  brick for walls

* Thatch and, later,
  tiles for roof

Originally widely distributed across the entire north German plain, Hallenhäuser still survive in many German villages.

EASTERN
NETHERLANDS/
NORTHERN GERMANY

TYPICAL HALLENHAUS

This is a typical style of Hallenhaus, a wood-frame house barn of which numerous fine examples still survive. Walls are made of brick or wattle and daub.

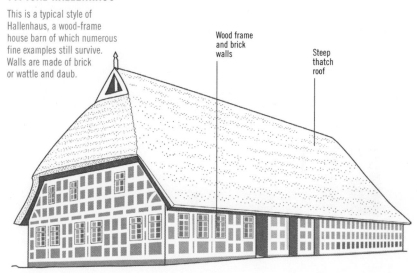

Wood frame and brick walls

Steep thatch roof

CROSS SECTION

This cross section of a large Hallenhaus clearly shows the roof space filled with a harvest of grain sacks; but why would farmers go to the inconvenience of storing the harvest in the rafters in this way? According to author and photographer Will Pryce, in the Middle Ages harvest time was set for a whole village, regardless of the weather. As a result, the corn had to be stored damp. The advantage of using the roof space in this manner was that smoke from the domestic fires below dried out the corn and prevented it from rotting.

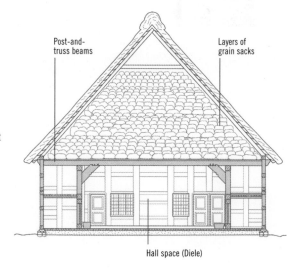

Post-and-truss beams

Layers of grain sacks

Hall space (Diele)

EARLY DUTCH WINDMILLS

One of the world's most remarkable vernacular structures is the windmill, a work of supreme craftsmanship and ingenuity, combining structural beauty with mechanical skill. Although found scattered in smaller numbers throughout much of Europe and Eurasia, it is in the Netherlands that the windmill has become a symbol of the country itself and where the greatest number was built in a relatively small area. Many survive in excellent condition, and a considerable number are still working today.

Windmills are said to have existed in the Netherlands from about 1200; the oldest known written reference dates from 1274. These were post mills (of two types, open and closed), and were used solely for grinding corn. From the post mills evolved the hollow-post wip mill, a drainage mill, first recorded in 1414. As the technology of these windmills steadily improved, they became larger, their water-lifting capacity increased, and they became more numerous.

Around 1526, the wip mill was replaced by the familiar large octagonal smock mill. This was topped by a rotating roof or cap containing a winch that could be turned to bring the sails into the wind; in the late 1500s, smock mills with tail poles were developed, enabling the sails to be turned from ground level. The span of the sails (twice the length of a single sail) was limited to 90–100 feet (27–30.5 m) by the length of the tree trunks of which they were made.

These smock mills were used not only for water drainage, but also for a variety of other industrial purposes—for hulling barley and rice, and for grinding cocoa, snuff, pepper, mustard, and other foodstuffs. They were also paper mills, oil mills, dye mills, and industrial mills for grinding chalk, lime, and oak bark for the tanneries. Special sawmills (*paltrokmolens* in Dutch) were also developed. In the seventeeth century, the Netherlands' "Golden Age," the industrial mill district of Zaan, north of Amsterdam, had nine hundred mills working day and night.

SEE ALSO

> Later Dutch Windmills, pages 60–61

> Iranian Desert Towns, pages 82–83

> Paisa House, pages 146–47

> Toraja Tongkonan, pages 158–59

The Netherlands is often called Holland, but the country consists of twelve provinces, of which the largest are North and South Holland. The country as a whole was only known as the Kingdom of Holland for a brief period from 1806 to 1810.

THE NETHERLANDS

MATERIALS

* Brick or stone base
* Wood structures throughout
* Canvas for sails

POST MILL

A side elevation of a post mill, the earliest type of mill recorded in use in the province of Holland in the thirteenth century, used for grinding corn. In those days, to ensure an uninterrupted supply of flour for the population, there had to be one windmill for every two thousand inhabitants.

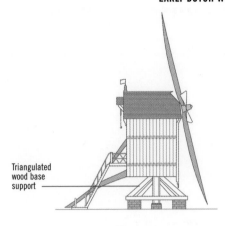

Triangulated wood base support

HOLLOW-POST WIP MILL

A side elevation of a hollow-post mill. These were the first windmills that used the power of the wind to drive a scoop wheel (later an Archimedes screw) to drain water from the land.

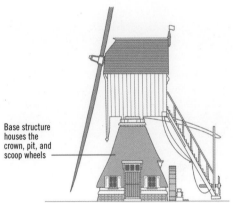

Base structure houses the crown, pit, and scoop wheels

SMOCK MILL

This is a large octagonal smock drainage mill of the South Holland type, with an internal scoop wheel. The smock mill gets its name because its tapered wood tower, clapboarded horizontally, resembles a peasant's smock.

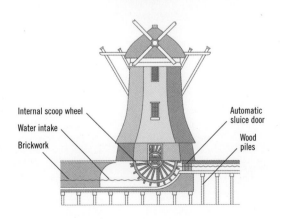

Internal scoop wheel

Water intake

Brickwork

Automatic sluice door

Wood piles

LATER DUTCH WINDMILLS

The round brick-built tower windmills were developed to give millers more working and storage space, and were originally situated on the outskirts of towns and villages. These wall mills *(walmolens)* were expanded into taller versions—often more than 100 feet (30.5 m) high—that were able to catch the wind across other buildings and thus could be built in the town's center.

Because of their great height, it was necessary to add halfway up the structure a circular wood "stage" with handrail to enable the miller to reach the sails and operate the break rope and the mill's winding mechanism for turning the cap.

These giant mills were suited for milling corn because they had as many as six or seven floors, each being used for a separate part of the milling process. First the grain was hoisted up in sacks from the grain store to the bin floor, through double-flap trapdoors, by means of a sack hoist driven by wind power. The grain then flowed by gravity from the hoppers (funnel-shape containers) to the stone floor, where it was ground. On the meal floor below, the flour was collected in sacks, which were then stored in the floor below.

At its base, a tower mill was some 30 feet (9 m) in diameter, thus providing a reasonable amount of living quarters for the miller and his family on the first two floors. Two pairs of stable doors facing each other enabled a horse and cart to deliver grain and take away the flour to the miller's customers. Between the bin floor and the cap was the dust floor, full of smoke, dripping oil, and dust from the grain.

By the nineteenth century there were as many as nine thousand windmills in the Netherlands, but their numbers declined rapidly during this period as steam power took over from wind as industry's main motive force. Many mills were demolished or neglected until conservation efforts began in the 1920s. Today, around 1,200 of the original mills survive; in addition, derelict mills are being restored and replica mills are being built on historical mill sites.

SEE ALSO

> Early Dutch Windmills, pages 58–59

The Netherlands is still famous for its windmills, of which some 1,200 survive to this day. They are used traditionally for draining water and grinding corn.

THE NETHERLANDS

MATERIALS

* Brick or stone base
* Wood structures throughout
* Canvas for sails

TOWER MILL

The world's tallest tower mills can be found in Schiedam, South Holland. *De Nolet*, a modern mill built in 2006 to generate electricity for a distillery, is 140 feet (42.5 m) to the cap. The second tallest is *De Noord*, a corn mill built in 1803 and still in use today, which is 109 feet (33.5 m) to the cap. This section view of a tower mill gives a clear view of all the levels and working parts.

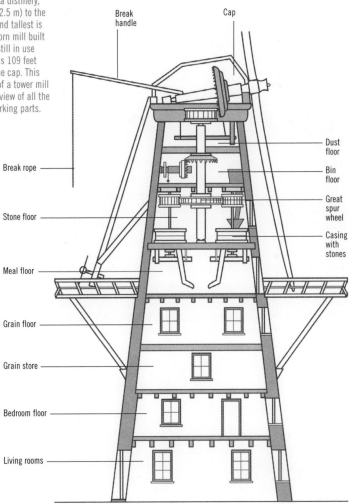

Break handle

Cap

Break rope

Stone floor

Meal floor

Grain floor

Grain store

Bedroom floor

Living rooms

Dust floor

Bin floor

Great spur wheel

Casing with stones

RUSSIAN IZBA

The traditional Russian *izba* (pl. *izby*), a "peasant house" built of interlocking ax-hewn logs, was for centuries the most widespread form of house found in the Russian countryside. A typical farmstead would consist of an izba, a log-built barn and hay shed, either attached to or separated from the main building, and a kitchen garden. Izby were constructed in many shapes and sizes, but they shared similar internal layouts. Broadly speaking, three main regional types of izba have been identified, which were designed to deal with different climatic and environmental conditions.

In the heavily forested north, izby tended to be larger and their farm buildings were arranged around a courtyard in an *L* or *U* shape. Due to the severe climate, another common northern form was the two-story *koshel* ("basket house"), in which the living quarters and agricultural spaces were integrated into one building, covered by an asymmetrical roof with a short, steep slope over the main house and a longer slope covering an interior yard and farm structures. Central Russian izby were smaller, with either attached or separate storage sheds and animal shelters; izby in southern Russia usually lacked basements and had similar farm structures around them.

Izby were constructed using hand axes, adzes, or knives, but not saws, and wood pegs rather than nails (metal was expensive). Building one was a communal effort, celebrated with feasts that were held at significant stages in the construction process. A great deal of attention was paid to the correct siting of the house; coins, wool, and frankincense were placed underneath the corners of the house so that its inhabitants would be healthy and wealthy. In one corner of the izba, the family's icons would be displayed, providing a spiritual focus for the home. Most surviving izby, some up to five hundred years old, are now found only in outdoor museums.

SEE ALSO

> Log Cabin,
  pages 132–33

> Zafimaniry House,
  pages 114–15

MATERIALS

* Interlocking ax-hewn logs

* Wood for roofing, although modern materials, including felting and corrugated iron, were used later

Widespread throughout Russia, wood izby made good use of the huge timber resources of this vast country.

RUSSIA

SMALL IZBA

This is an example of the smaller form of izba found in southern or central Russia, built of fir or pinewood. A small traditional village would consist of a number of izbas, a church, a bathhouse, windmills, storage sheds, and other outbuildings, spaced apart to try to prevent the spread of fire.

Wood roof

Log construction with interlocking corners

IZBA HEATING

Keeping warm in an izba in winter was a major problem and one traditional solution was a "Russian stove" known as a *pech*, a brick masonry construction used for cooking meals, baking bread and pies, drying out grains, mushrooms, and roots, and for heating and drying the house.

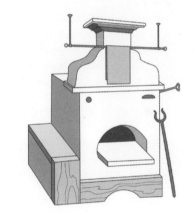

DECORATION

In the north and in the Volga area, many izby were highly decorated with exterior carvings that embellished the eaves, window frames, and balcony; interiors were often brightly painted. The house was considered a cosmos unto itself; its facade was likened to a human face.

FROM DUTCH WINDMILLS TO GERMAN BARNS
WOOD CHURCHES

The wood churches of Eastern and Central Europe are found across a vast region encompassing northern Russia and Finland, Poland, Czechoslovakia, Romania, Hungary, and the Balkans. They were built in many shapes and styles, but share the same basic forms of log construction, which were also used in wood houses. Three distinctive forms of wood church, found in the Ukraine and adjacent areas of Poland and Slovakia, were built by three different ethnic groups—the Boyko, Lemko, and Hutsul people—who stem originally from the Carpathian highlands.

The Boyko ranged mainly across large parts of the Carpathians in the Ukraine, as well as adjacent areas of northeast Slovakia and southeast Poland. Today, Boyko in the Ukraine consider themselves Ukrainian, and most belong to the Ukraine Greek Catholic Church. The Lemko, according to *The Encyclopedia of Vernacular Architecture*, were "once cattle-breeding nomads coming from the east in the fourteenth and fifteenth centuries. In the nineteenth century, they changed their lifestyle, developing agriculture, and exploiting forests." The semi-nomadic Hutsul live in an area that spans from southeast of the Boyko territory to the Romanian segment of Carpathia. There are competing hypotheses as to their origins and identity. Some say the name Hutsul derives from *hotul,* the Romanian word for "thief"; others that it stems from *kochul,* the Slavic word for "wanderer."

The Boyko churches consist of three log rooms built along an east–west axis, each topped by a dome. The churches of the Lemko people followed the same three-part structure on an east–west axis. The churches of the Hutsul are also built on an east–west axis, but are formed of five rooms, with a dominant central square nave and two-storeyed rectangular rooms connected to it on all four sides.

These treasures of vernacular architecture are slowly attracting attention internationally; they have become important symbols for the ethnic peoples whose identity was lost during the Soviet era.

SEE ALSO

> Wood Churches of Chiloé, pages 150–51

> The Great Mosque of Djenné, pages 104–5

The Carpathian Mountains form an arc of 932 miles (1,500 km) across Central and Eastern Europe, including the Ukraine.

THE UKRAINE

MATERIALS

* Logs to make the wood structures

* Wood shingles for roofs

BOYKO CHURCH

In the three-room, three-dome Boyko churches, the central room—the nave—is the largest, and has the largest dome above it. To the east side is the sanctuary, to the west the *narthex* or *babinec*, where the women sat; these rooms are smaller, with smaller domes above. The churches are encircled by a wide overhanging porch, covered with notched shingles and supported by posts.

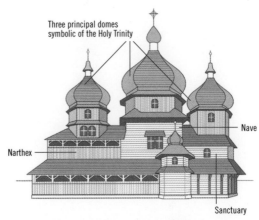

Three principal domes symbolic of the Holy Trinity

Narthex

Nave

Sanctuary

LEMKO CHURCH

Here we see the basic structure of a Lemko church, with the small presbytery at the east, the larger square nave in the center, and the narthex on the west. The presbytery is topped by a rising series of progressively smaller roofs, culminating in a dome and a cross; the nave by a larger, higher version of the same. The narthex has an even taller bell tower over it, which contains a storage room on the second floor.

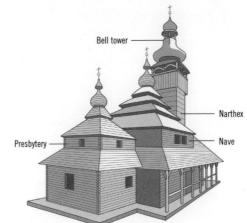

Bell tower

Narthex

Nave

Presbytery

HUTSUL CHURCH

All five rooms of the Hutsul church are covered with gable roofs with a small cupola on top. The central room slopes upward to form an octagon, covered by an eight-sided conical roof. In such Hutsul churches there were two entrances—one on the western side for women, the other on the southern side for men.

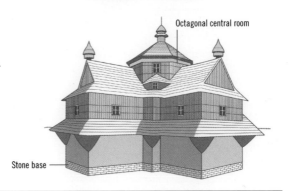

Octagonal central room

Stone base

SLOVENIAN HAYRACK AND BEE HOUSE

Two vernacular structures have become important symbols of Slovenian culture: the hayrack *(kozolec)* and the bee house *(ulnjaki)*. The former are not unique to Slovenia, but are found there in large numbers; the latter incorporate a technical innovation in beekeeping and also serve as a vehicle for an important folk art tradition. The landscape of Slovenia—a small country bordering Italy, Austria, and Croatia—is studded with tens of thousands of kozolecs. First documented in 1689, they are now built using modern materials, but still resonate as a symbol of the Slovene nation. Dr. Borut Juvanec of Lubliana University has said: "It is the only ethnical architecture I know."

Beekeeping has been practiced in Slovenia for more than six hundred years and the bee houses are unique wood structures, topped with a thatch or shingle roof, that form another distinctive feature of the Slovenian landscape. These structures evolved as a protective shelter for numerous drawer-shaped hives, an invention of the painter and beekeeper Anton Janša, which were stacked together in blocks kept in the bee house's side.

A tradition of decorating the spruce panels at the end of the drawers with religious, historical, and humorous paintings developed among beekeepers in one area of the country, and this practice spread throughout Slovenia. The oldest surviving bee-panel painting is dated 1758; the heyday of the practice was the period from 1820 to 1880, and it was widespread until the end of World War I. More than six hundred different designs have been recorded, many of which are preserved in the Museum of Apiculture in Radovljica. They are now highly valued and considered among the most important works of Slovene folk art. Bee houses in many shapes and forms persist in modern times, as do the painted hives—which sport modern, vividly colored illustrations.

SEE ALSO

> Ganvié Stilt Village, pages 108–9

The republic of Slovenia touches the Alps in the north and borders the Mediterranean in the south.

SLOVENIA

MATERIALS

* Wood for racks, roof, beehive structure, and drawers

* Straw, wood shingles, or clay tiles for roof

HAYRACK (KOZOLEC)

The simplest type of kozolec is a freestanding wood rack with a roof, for drying hay and grain. This would be used on steep slopes and plains, anchored with supports, if necessary; in wet areas it has a projecting roof on one side to provide shelter from sudden downpours.

LINKED HAYRACK (TOPLAR)

Standing on wood legs, with a drying rack attached to either side, the larger, more elaborate and beautiful form is called a *toplar* or "linked hayrack." Its second floor, principally a storage room, is reached by a staircase and fronted by a balcony. Its substantial overhanging roof is either thatched with straw or covered with wood shingles or clay tiles.

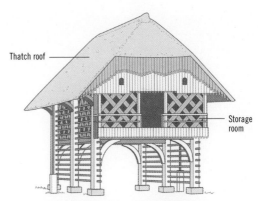

Thatch roof

Storage room

BEE HOUSE (ULNJAKI)

This beautiful and ornate bee house is made entirely of wood with a shingle roof. The hive drawers can be seen stacked in the front, many of which are painted in bright colors and illustrated with folk art. Many of these huts were mobile, enabling bee colonies to be moved from pasture to pasture.

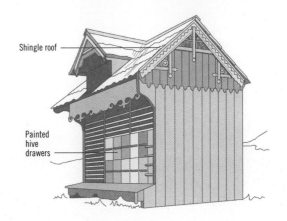

Shingle roof

Painted hive drawers

FROM MEDITERRANEAN CAVES
TO BEDOUIN TENTS

The Mediterranean is ringed with cave dwellings and cave houses of various forms, many of which have ancient roots. Dry-stone architecture is another widespread building type, most beautifully expressed in the trulli of southern Italy. The ubiquitous black tent serves not only the Bedouins, but nomadic groups across a huge area of northern Africa, the Middle East, and beyond. It survives in the modern age, unlike the reed houses of the Marsh Arabs of Iraq, whose whole culture is under threat. The impressive earth towers of Yemen and the ingenious wind catchers of Iran offer lessons for modern architects seeking to build in hot, inclement climates where water is scarce.

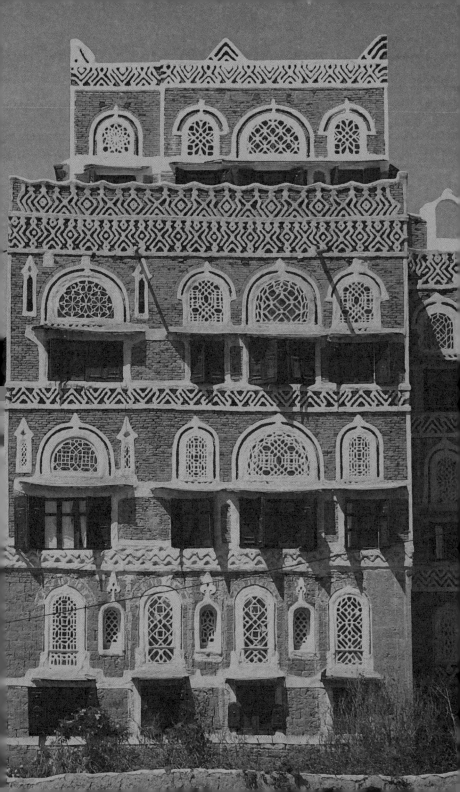

TRULLO STONE HOUSE

Based on a prehistoric building technique, dry-stone houses with conical roofs are found throughout the Mediterranean region and beyond. They follow similar construction principles, but each type has its own name and style. The *trullo* (pl. *trulli*) is the name for such buildings that are found scattered throughout the countryside of the Itria Valley of the Apulia region of southeast Italy. The trulli built in this region are either rectangular structures with truncated pyramid roofs or circular structures with ogival (pointed) roofs. The only concentrations of trulli are found in the Monti and Aja Piccola quarters of Alberobello, now a UNESCO World Heritage Site, which contain more than 1,600 in all, the majority of which are privately owned and still inhabited. The trulli here are distinctive rectangular-plan buildings, containing several square rooms with conical roofs, connected by semicircular arches.

These trulli are constructed out of roughly worked limestone boulders, collected from neighboring fields, and were built, without foundations, directly on the underlying natural rock, using the dry-stone technique (without mortar). The double walls that form the rectangular rooms have rubble cores, are pierced by small windows, and rise to a height of 5–6 feet (1.5–1.8 m). These walls are extremely thick, providing a cool environment in hot weather and insulating against the cold in the winter.

The conical roofs, which also have double layers, spring directly from the walls and are built up of successive courses of overlapping gray limestone slabs, 2–2¾ inches (5–7 cm) thick, known as *chiance* or *chiancarelle*. When complete, the cones are sealed off with a plastered "hat," culminating in a pinnacle. The interiors are equipped with wood fittings, such as door frames and barrel-vault niches. In some of the larger trulli there is a second story formed from a wood floor and reached by means of a wood staircase.

SEE ALSO

> Mousgoum Tolek, pages 106–7

> Indian Stepped Ponds and Stepwells, pages 98–99

MATERIALS

* Limestone boulders and rubble for double walls

* Gray limestone slabs (chincarelle) to construct conical roofs

* Wood for door frames, barrel-vault niches, floors, and staircases

Apulia is the least mountainous region of Italy, mainly covered by broad plains and low-lying hills, with a very dry climate.

APULIA REGION, SOUTHEAST ITALY

GROUND-FLOOR CONSTRUCTION

This is the first stage in the construction of a four-room Alberobello trullo. Here we see the ground-floor construction level. The basic walls have been built and a flat roof, with circular openings, has been completed. Note the main arched entrance and the narrow stone steps leading up to the roof.

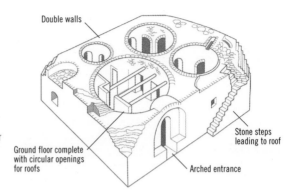

Double walls

Ground floor complete with circular openings for roofs

Arched entrance

Stone steps leading to roof

ROOF CONSTRUCTION

Here three conical roofs of various sizes have been built using the technique known as corbeling, the laying of successive courses of stones, each projecting slightly inward over the preceding ones. The more pointed chimney on the far left carries away smoke and fumes from fireplaces and ovens.

Pointed chimney

Corbeled conical roof made of limestone slabs

COMPLETED TRULLO

This finished trullo has an additional room to the side. Two of the conical roofs are topped with a decorative pinnacle called a *cucurneoi* or *tintinule*; one is marked with a whitewashed cross—the unpainted roofs were often marked with mythological or religious symbols. A final roof covering links the various parts of the building together.

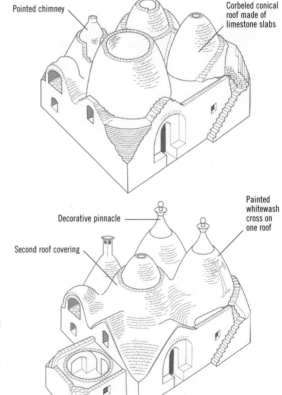

Decorative pinnacle

Second roof covering

Painted whitewash cross on one roof

MEDITERRANEAN CAVE DWELLINGS

The Mediterranean region is one of the major concentrations of cave dwellings in the world, some of which have been continually inhabited since ancient times. The earliest man-made horizontal caves in the region have been found by archaeologists in Anatolia and the neighboring Aegean islands. According to historian A. T. Luttrell, "Mediterranean people have always chosen caves and grottoes, natural or excavated, as providing cool and often defensible dwellings, stores, stalls, cisterns, churches, burial places, and catacombs."

Vertical caves exist in other parts of the western Mediterranean and in southern France; horizontal caves in Spain, Italy, Greece, Morocco, and many of the Mediterranean islands, including Sicily and Malta, where evidence of cave dwelling dates as far back as 5000 BC. Their distribution is largely conditioned by geology, being built or excavated in areas where limestone, sandstone, or volcanic deposits (especially tufa) are the predominant rock.

Three sites are of particular interest: the *Sassi* of Matera in southern Italy, the cave houses of northern Andalusia in Spain, and the extraordinary cave houses and underground cities of Cappadocia in Turkey. The Sassi of Matera cave complex in southern Italy is the most outstanding and intact example of a troglodyte settlement in the whole of Europe, dating from the Paleolithic onwards. It is carved out of the local tufa stone.

One of the major concentrations of cave dwellings in Spain can be found in the mountains of the Altiplano (High Plateau) of northern Andalusia. The rock formations in this area consist of a sedimentary sandstone composed of alternate layers of hard and soft rock. The hard rock is impervious to water and provides a secure roof; the soft rock could be dug out by hand. There are caves here that date back to the Iron Age, thousands of which later provided homes for farmworkers and their families, until seventy-five percent of them left in the late 1960s when the local economy collapsed.

SEE ALSO

> Cappadocian Cave Dwellings, pages 74–75

> Chinese Yao Dong, pages 90–91

MATERIALS

* Carved out of limestone, sandstone, or volcanic deposits, such as tufa

* Brick frontage and later extensions

* Wood for internal/external joinery

A tradition of cave and pit dwellings has survived in many countries around the Mediterranean.

FRANCE/ITALY/
SPAIN/GREECE/
NORTH AFRICA

SASSI OF MATERA

The Sassi of Matera is a network of cave houses interlinked with buildings above them in a spontaneous and haphazard manner. During the 1950s, due to its neglected condition, the whole complex was closed, and its twenty thousand inhabitants were moved to other areas. The abandoned houses became the property of the state and a wall was erected to prevent them from being occupied. Then, in 1986, the Italian government allocated 100 billion lira to reclaim the unique complex, and in 1993 it was declared a UNESCO World Heritage Site.

TYPICAL CAVE HOUSE

This is the kitchen of the reconstructed interior of a typical cave house in Vico Solitario in the Sasso Caveoso neighborhood of Matera. In recent years, some three thousand people have returned to live in cave homes, and Matera has become a center for international tourism.

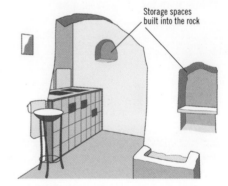

Storage spaces built into the rock

ANDALUSIAN CAVE HOUSE

In the last ten years in Andalusia, there has been a substantial revival in the popularity of caves as both vacation and permanent homes. Many renovated cave houses have had some form of external building added to the front of the cave, as seen here.

CAPPADOCIAN CAVE DWELLINGS

The Turkish region of Cappadocia, in the center of Anatolia, contains the most spectacular examples of cave houses and underground dwellings in the world. Its landscape was formed from a layer of tufa between 328 and 492 feet (100 and 150 m) thick, from the ashes produced by the three volcanoes in the region, which are presently inactive. Over the centuries this has been carved into unusual shapes and forms by the action of wind and water.

The most striking features in the Cappadocia region are the geological forms known as "fairy chimneys" (*peri bacalari*). Giant pinnacles of eroded softer rock topped by a cap of harder rock, these extraordinary natural structures have been inhabited for centuries. Inside some are five-story houses with rooms, staircases, and windows hand-carved out of the soft volcanic rock.

The first cave settlements here date back to the early days of Christianity, when Christian settlers, needing to hide from invading Arabic and Persian troops, dug out and carved underground towns. There are no fewer than thirty-six of these towns in this area, the largest being at Derinkuyu, which housed between ten and twenty thousand people. A 5½-mile (9-km) tunnel connected Derinkuyu with the second-largest underground city at Kaymakly, of which four levels of an estimated eleven have been excavated thus far.

More than four hundred Christian monasteries, churches, and chapels were also carved from the rock in Cappadocia—the largest is Tokali church, which contains paintings depicting the life of Jesus. In most of the Cappadocian villages the older dwellings are part cave, part house. The family retreats to the warmer cave rooms in winter and lives in the attached arch houses in the summer. The cave rooms were also used throughout the year for food storage. Other buildings—stables, pigeon coops, bee houses, and cloakrooms—were added to form a domestic complex surrounded by a protective wall.

SEE ALSO

> Mediterranean Cave Dwellings, pages 72–73

MATERIALS

* Carved out of limestone, sandstone, or volcanic deposits, such as tufa

* Brick frontage and later extensions

* Wood for internal/external joinery

The ancient region of Cappadocia in central Turkey is a place of exceptional natural wonders.

CAPPADOCIA, TURKEY

FAIRY CHIMNEYS

The fairy chimneys (peri bacalari) of Cappadocia are extraordinary natural features that have been turned into habitations. Inside some are five-story houses with rooms, staircases, and windows hand-carved out of the soft volcanic rock. The cap of volcanic basalt rock protects the cone of tufa beneath it from erosion.

UNDERGROUND CITY

Derinkuyu in Cappadocia was found, by chance, under a hill, and opened to the public in 1965. It covers an area of 1½ square miles (4 sq km) and consists of seven levels, extending to a depth of 229–79 feet (70–85 m). It contains some two thousand households and an extensive network of subterranean facilities, including stables for horses, wine cellars, water wells, and churches.

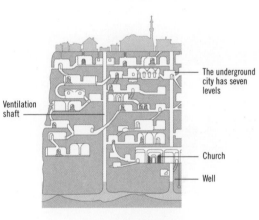

Ventilation shaft

The underground city has seven levels

Church

Well

CAVE DWELLING

A part cave, part dwelling in Cappadocia. Since the 1970s the Turkish government has tried to resettle cave dwellers in more modern accommodation, but many have returned to their original dwellings, which are much better suited to the climate. Cappadocia is now a major tourist attraction, and many caves have been renovated as hotels and boarding houses for visitors.

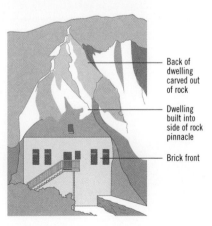

Back of dwelling carved out of rock

Dwelling built into side of rock pinnacle

Brick front

BLACK TENTS

The black tent in its various forms is used by nomadic groups across a huge area, from Mauritania in the west to the Tibetan plateau in the far east, most of which is within a climatic region characterized by hot, arid, or semiarid conditions. It can be found in all the Arabic Mediterranean nations, in the Middle East and Afghanistan. This form of shelter is used by the Romany in parts of Europe, by the Yuruks and Kurds of Turkey, the Baluch of Pakistan, and, most famously, by the Bedouin. For all these peoples and many others, the black tent provides shade and protection against wind, sand, and dust.

The main structure of the tent is a varying arrangement of poles, secured by ropes and pegs, overlaid by a covering made of black goat hair (preferred because it is darker and thicker than sheep's wool). "Black tent dwellers are weavers," writes Torvald Faegre in *Tents: Architecture of the Nomads.* "They weave not only the roofs, walls, and floors of their homes, but many of the furnishings as well."

The Bedouin call their tent *bait al Sha'ar* ("house of hair") and it is considered by many to be the form most perfectly adapted to the desert environment. The main cover consists of a number of broad strips of cloth that are sewn together to form a great rectangle, 98–131 feet (30–40 m) in length, which is then draped over ropes and supported by poles. The ropes carry the load to the stakes, which lend tension to the structure and anchor it. A long narrow strip of cloth is attached to three sides of the tent using wood pins and draped to the ground. The remaining open side always faces away from the wind; it is also covered with cloth if the nights are cold.

The interior is divided up by decorated curtains to form two main sections—the male quarters on one side, which also serves as the public area, and the kitchen and women's quarters on the other.

SEE ALSO

> Mongolian Ger,
  pages 94–95

> Yanomami Shabano,
  pages 144–45

> Aboriginal Shelter,
  pages 164–65

The Bedouin, an Arabic ethnic group, are found throughout the desert belt that runs from the Atlantic coast to the Middle East.

**BEDOUIN REGION,
NORTH AFRICA/
MIDDLE EAST**

MATERIALS

* Wood poles, secured
  by hemp ropes and
  wood pegs

* Cloth, woven from
  black goat hair

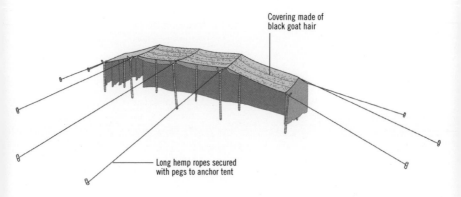

Covering made of
black goat hair

Long hemp ropes secured
with pegs to anchor tent

BEDOUIN TENT

The distinctive features of
the Bedouin tent are its long
flattened roof, which has
an aerodynamic profile that
lessens wind resistance, and its
extremely long tent ropes, made
of hemp, which are stretched out
horizontally and act like a ship's
anchor. They are fastened to the
ground by wood pegs.

Flat roof lessens
wind resistance

INSIDE THE TENT

These side and bird's-eye
views of the Bedouin black
tent show clearly the three
almost equal sections—an open
entrance area at one end, the
male quarters in the middle, and
the female quarters at the other
end. The side curtains can be
rolled up to provide ventilation.

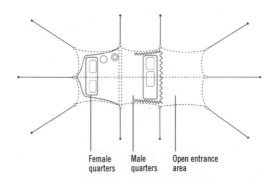

Female
quarters

Male
quarters

Open entrance
area

YEMEN TOWER HOUSE

Tower houses are a form of building unique to southern Arabia. They originated in pre-Islamic times in the south of Yemen, where tribal strife was the motivation for developing an effective way of building defensive towers out of local materials. From there, they spread across the country because they were an ideal solution for housing an extended family, because new stories could be added as the family group grew in size.

Most tower houses are at least five stories high, and some reach as many as eight or nine. The vertical arrangement follows an upward transition from public to private space. The internal layout of the tower house varies between town and country; each individual house has some variation in its particulars. In a rural area, the ground floor, apart from the entrance hall, is for animals and the storage of wood, fruit, and grain; in towns, it is used for shops and stores.

The main feature of the first floor is the rectangular public reception room *(diwan)* for visitors to the house. In typical Yemeni style, this is ringed by cushions, with a carpet in the center, and illuminated by windows that have shutters for ventilation in the bottom half and colored glass in the top. One level from the top is the kitchen with an adjacent outside terrace. This is the primary domain of the women of the house, who, after their labors, can relax on the terrace, which has high-screened walls. The highest level contains the *mufraj,* a private sitting room reserved for special guests and family members. The men gather here in the afternoon to exchange conversation, smoke their water pipes, chew fresh leaves of the *qat* plant, and listen to poetry or music.

The foundations of the tower houses are constructed using stone or earth (sun-dried clay, mud blocks, or fired bricks). In the city, the ground and first floors are made of tufa, and the upper floors of fired bricks. The facades of the houses are typically highly decorated, as are the windows and doors.

SEE ALSO

> Lhasa Buildings, pages 96–97

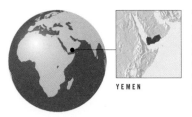

YEMEN

The Republic of Yemen, situated between Oman and Saudi Arabia, holds a strategic position on Bab el Mandeb, the strait linking the Red Sea and the Gulf of Aden, one of the world's most active shipping lanes.

MATERIALS

* Stone for the foundations

* Sun-dried clay, mud blocks, fired bricks, or tufa for walls

CROSS SECTION

A cross section of a tower house, which clearly shows a below-ground grain store, the arched entrance on the ground floor, the diwan on the first floor, three floors of storerooms, living and sleeping areas, the fifth-floor kitchen and terrace, with the mufraj on the top.

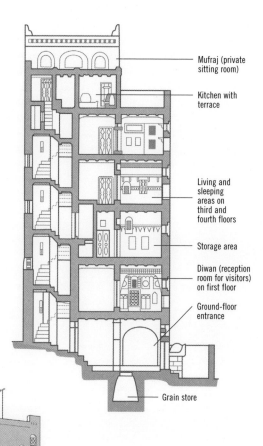

Mufraj (private sitting room)

Kitchen with terrace

Living and sleeping areas on third and fourth floors

Storage area

Diwan (reception room for visitors) on first floor

Ground-floor entrance

Grain store

CITY TOWER HOUSE

The defensive exterior of a city tower house, fourteen thousand of which can be seen in Sana'a, Yemen's capital and a UNESCO World Heritage Site. These houses are also found in Shibam, the "Manhattan of the desert," which has some five hundred towers made of straw-reinforced mud bricks—the tallest mud buildings in the world.

MARSH ARAB REED HOUSE

For millennia the extensive wilderness of marshland created by the confluence of the Tigris and Euphrates rivers has been inhabited by the Ma'dan people of southern Iraq, popularly known as the Marsh Arabs. They live on islands of reeds, on which they have built a variety of reed buildings, serving many different purposes, including cattle shelters, workshops, storerooms, and living quarters.

The construction of these reed buildings is an ancient craft. Long, thick bundles of reeds are set into holes in the reed bed, in two parallel rows some 6½ feet (2 m) apart; the tops are then bent over until they overlap, and then bound together to form a series of horseshoe-shaped arches. These are in turn linked together by long reed bundles that run in spaced horizontal rows along the length of the building. Set at each end are four taller vertical bundles of reeds (sometimes a palm trunk covered with reeds), which stick up higher than the main roofline. The roof of the structure is then covered with closely woven reed matting; the walls with a more open matting that enables a draft to flow through. Both ends are similarly covered with a mesh of open matting, with a large central opening at one or both ends. Inside the structure, bundles of reeds are used as backrests and to make beds, cots, and baskets, as well as reed mats to cover the floor. The fishermen use reeds to make their canoes and poles; the reed and its products are also used for trade.

The bottom of these buildings rots in seven to ten years, at which time the base is cut away and the building lowered, then used for a further period before being abandoned. Fewer and fewer of these buildings survive today because the life of the Marsh Arabs, and the marshes themselves, have been decimated. Saddam Hussein built numerous dams to drain them and succeeded in turning most of the area into a dry salt-encrusted wasteland. Some forty percent of marshland has since been reflooded.

SEE ALSO

> Ganvié Stilt Village,
  pages 108–9

> Toda Hut,
  pages 100–1

> Urus Reed House,
  pages 148–49

The marshlands of southern Iraq, the traditional home of the Ma'dan, are under threat due to water shortages.

SOUTHERN IRAQ

MATERIALS

* Reed bundles to form basic framework

* Reed matting to make roof and walls

MUDHIF FRAMEWORK

The largest reed buildings built by the Marsh Arabs are the cavernous cathedral-like *mudhifs,* originally constructed for their tribal leaders, later as guesthouses. The principles of the structure are the same as that of smaller houses, but on a much larger scale. Its five giant arches of reeds are strengthened at top and sides by long reed bundles.

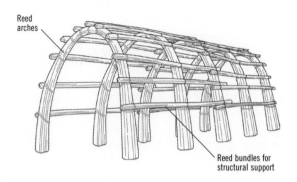

Reed arches

Reed bundles for structural support

REED-HOUSE WALLS

Here the woven reed matting has been added to form the walls. It is open in form to enable a draft to flow through in hot weather. Mudhifs were protected by being built up on a bank of woven reeds to raise them above the waterways.

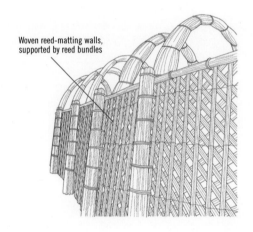

Woven reed-matting walls, supported by reed bundles

COMPLETED REED HOUSE

The finished mudhif, complete with giant reed towers and an impressive facade. They date back to the Sumerian age (*c.* 2900–2350 BC). The Ma'dan continued to build them until the 1990s, when three hundred thousand of them died or fled their homes due to Saddam Hussein's campaign of repression.

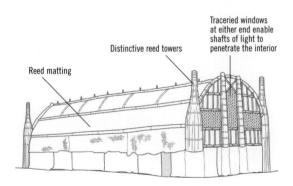

Reed matting

Distinctive reed towers

Traceried windows at either end enable shafts of light to penetrate the interior

IRANIAN DESERT TOWNS

Life in the desert towns and cities of Iran is dominated by the scorching sun, by the ongoing threat of sandstorms, by ferocious winds, and by the need for water. These climatic conditions have shaped the whole construction of these conurbations and led to a unique vernacular style as well as some extraordinary innovations, including ingenious underground water-supply systems, known as *qanats,* that are still in use today. Inside these towns there is a carefully planned maze of narrow and irregular streets and a web of closely interconnected lofty buildings, enclosed from all directions. This prevents sandstorms from entering the town, reducing wind speed, and stops the sun from penetrating the streets.

Residential buildings are adobe constructions with thick walls made of muddy unbaked bricks, the only building material available. These rise up to 20 feet (6 m) tall, with domes and arched roofs, and are built facing the direction of the rising sun and the blowing wind. Inside, the ground floor is a little below the street, with the first-floor living quarters 10–13 feet (3–4 m) above it.

To make the house habitable under all conditions presented a challenge to the original builders, who lacked modern heating and cooling equipment. The thick walls serve the house well during the winter, absorbing the heat and preserving it for eight hours, releasing it at night to keep the house warm. In the summer, the absorbed temperature causes problems, which led to the invention of ingenious systems using air traps (also known as wind catchers) linked to a ventilator duct and a water reservoir.

The foremost example of this desert architecture is the ancient city of Yadz. It is not only one of the largest cities in the world built almost entirely out of adobe, but also has the largest network of qanats in the world and a considerable number of impressive wind catchers, including one of the tallest, and one of the few examples of a double wind tower in the world.

SEE ALSO

> Indian Stepped Ponds and Stepwells, pages 98–99

> Great Mosque of Djenné, pages 104–5

> New Mexican Adobe House, pages 136–37

MATERIALS

* Unbaked mud bricks to build thick walls; more recently, fired brick

* Wood for internal joinery

* Glazed decorative tiling for internal walls and ceilings

Much of Iran is desert. The central "Salt Desert" is mostly uninhabited. The eastern Lout desert can be one of the hottest and driest spots on the planet.

IRAN/
SURROUNDING
AREAS

COURTYARD HOUSE

This cross section of a typical Yadz courtyard house shows how the wind is captured and funneled down a long shaft, from rooftop to basement, creating air flows through the living quarters and over a cold-water pool.

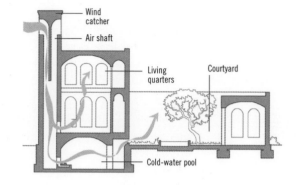

Wind catcher

Air shaft

Living quarters

Courtyard

Cold-water pool

WIND CATCHER

Wind towers or "catchers" of many types are found in desert regions across the Middle East and beyond. In Iran, wind catchers take the form of a four-sided capped tower, with ducts on each side that can be closed or opened, depending on the wind's direction. These can bring cool fresh air into the house and expel stale hot air, helping to make the house habitable in all seasons.

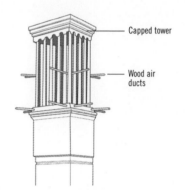

Capped tower

Wood air ducts

ORNATE WIND TOWERS

The ornate Khāné-ye Borūjerdīhā or "Borujerdis' House" is a famous historical house in Kashan, Iran, considered one of the gems of Persian residential architecture. The house, which took eighteen years to build, using 150 craftsmen, has three 131-foot (40-m)-tall wind towers (two pictured), which keep the interior unusually cool.

FROM JAPANESE MINKA
TO TODA HUTS

The beautiful traditional building and woodworking skills of Japan are highlighted in our profiles of townhouses and urban minkas. We investigate the extraordinary Chinese yao dong, which are either sunk in pits or dug out of cliffsides, and the impressive tulou of Fujian, fortified buildings large enough to hold an entire clan of people. On the roof of the world, we visit the gers of Mongolia, supreme examples of nomadic shelter, and celebrate the conservation and the restoration of some remarkable buildings in old Lhasa, Tibet. India's wealth of vernacular structures is represented by the impressive stepped ponds and stepwells of Rajasthan and the barrel-vault huts of the much-studied Toda people in the south.

JAPANESE MINKA

Minka is a broad term that literally means "houses of the people" and covers a wide variety of residential types, from the great houses of village headmen and merchants to the smaller dwellings of the poorest farmers. Minka can also be classified into two main groups: farmhouses *(noka)* and townhouses *(machiya)*. There were different styles for each region of Japan, shaped by the terrain and climate, varying from the steep thatched roofs of the north that could cope with heavy winter snows, to smaller, lower buildings in the south with raised floors to maximize ventilation and minimize flood damage.

Noka were constructed from local materials. The basic skeletal structure that formed the roof and walls and the posts that carried all the weight of the building were made of wood. Stone was used for the foundations. The external, nonload-bearing walls of the noka were made of bamboo and clay. The internal space was divided up by sliding wood and paper screens *(fusuma)* or wood lattice doors. The roof was mainly thatched with grass or straw, occasionally with clay roofing tiles for status.

The Japanese painter Mukai Junkichi (1901–1995) devoted a large part of his life to capturing the traditional thatched minka on canvas in the period after World War II, at a time when many were abandoned and fell into disrepair in the countryside, or were demolished to make space for modern buildings in the cities.

Nowadays, minka are considered historical landmarks and are preserved by national and local governments; many of them survive only in Folk Building parks. The Historic Villages of Shirakawa-gō and Gokayama have been designated a UNESCO World Heritage Site and contain some marvelous minka built with steep, sloping roofs in the style known as *gasshō-zukuri* ("prayer-hand construction"). These large three- or four-story houses were built to accommodate extended families and, on the upper floors, silkworm factories.

SEE ALSO

> Japanese
  Townhouse,
  pages 88–89

> Hallenhaus
  House Barn,
  pages 56–57

> Zafimaniry House,
  pages 114–15

MATERIALS

* Lumber for wood-
  frame load-bearing
  structure

* Bamboo and clay
  for walls

* Wood and paper
  screens to divide
  internal space

* Thatch of grass
  or straw for roof;
  the alternative is
  clay tiles

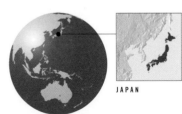

Minka are found scattered throughout Japan in urban and rural areas. The UNESCO World Heritage Site is in the Japanese alps on the main island of Honshu.

JAPAN

GASSHŌ-ZUKURI

An example of the gasshō-zukuri (steep-slope roof) style of minka, its extensive voluminous thatch being designed to cope with heavy snowfalls. Its sturdy wood frame was also earthquake resistant. Often three to five stories high, it was fronted by a broad veranda, the internal space being divided by bamboo screens. Minka were not the most comfortable of dwellings, particularly in winter, because the only heating came from an inefficient, smoky cooking hearth.

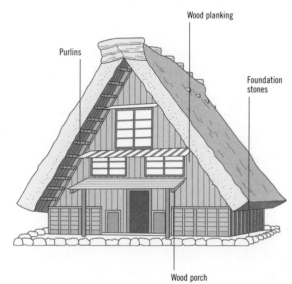

Purlins

Wood planking

Foundation stones

Wood porch

CROSS SECTION

This cross section shows the internal structure of a gasshō-zukuri. The master bedrooms were situated on the right, the living areas on the left. The thatched roof is bound to bamboo laths and rafters. Above, great hand-hewn beams of pine, zelkova, or chestnut stretch across the main expanse of the building, connecting the outer framework of the minka to the interior posts.

Ridge structure

Grass or straw thatch

Structural framing

Roof supports

Extended eaves

Internal screens

Foundation (platform/wood supports)

JAPANESE TOWNHOUSE

Japan has always had a ready supply of wood, so it is a natural choice for a building material. The wood house shown opposite is a nineteenth-century example of a sophisticated townhouse. Such houses are no longer common in modern Japan, and intact examples are carefully preserved. The more common type of traditional townhouse is the urban minka, known as the machiya, which is found throughout Japan, with the finest examples being in old Kyoto. These long narrow row houses, fronted with wood grilles, are built by first erecting wood columns on top of a flat foundation made of packed earth or stones. In order to avoid moisture from the ground, the floor is elevated and is laid across horizontal wood floor beams.

The frame is made of wood, and the house's weight is supported by vertical columns, horizontal beams and diagonal braces. The houses have a large sloping roof, covered with tiles called *kawara*, with deep eaves to protect the house from the hot summer sun. The frame of the house supports the weight of the roof. A typical house has two entrances, one private and one for guests. Inside is a guest room, a room for entertaining, one or two bedrooms, and a dining room, which is central and links to all the other rooms. The rooms are divided from each other by sliding screens. There are windows at front and back, but none on the side walls.

There are two or three tiny gardens, both inside and outside the house; if sprayed with water, these create cool breezes that help with summer temperatures. In addition, the kitchen ceiling reaches right up to the roof to a skylight, which enables hot air from the whole house to escape. Some areas of the have wood flooring while others are covered with *tatami,* mats made from woven rush grass. Traditionally, the exterior walls were made of woven bamboo plastered with earth on both sides, although modern materials, such as plywood, have often replaced this.

SEE ALSO

> Japanese Minka, pages 86–87

MATERIALS

* Wood for frame, floors, and internal structure

* Stone for supporting foundations

* Lime plaster, as a traditional finish for external walls

* Tile for roof (tiles made locally and fired)

* Paper for interior screens, dividing the spaces of the house

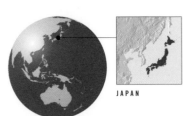

Traditional Japanese buildings made generous use of the country's woodlands and forests, which cover sixty-eight percent of the country.

JAPAN

TOWNHOUSE EXTERIOR

This house is an elegant variation on the basic rectangular, two-story, wood-frame Japanese vernacular form. Although it was built in the nineteenth century, its origins are much earlier. Additional verandas, and the wood fencing surrounding the compound it occupies, indicate that the house belongs to a wealthy family.

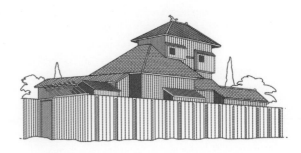

WOOD FRAMEWORK

Part of the house stripped to its wood framework, with a shallow-pitch roof and a veranda at one end. The framework rests on foundation supporting stones, sunk into the ground. Most of the rooms are floored with wood planks, although some, notably the kitchen and corridors, may have simple earthen floors.

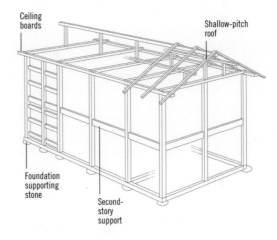

Ceiling boards

Shallow-pitch roof

Foundation supporting stone

Second-story support

CROSS SECTION

This cross section shows the veranda and guest room. Room division is movable, based on screens and sliding doors. The *shoji* is a wood-frame sliding door "glazed" with paper, and the *fusuma* is a sliding screen with translucent paper panes. Storage and shelving are built in. Room sizes are defined by the number of tatami mats each can contain; the typical tatami mat has a standard dimension of 6 x 3 feet (1.8 m x 90 cm).

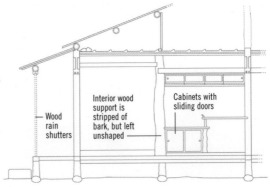

Wood rain shutters

Interior wood support is stripped of bark, but left unshaped

Cabinets with sliding doors

CHINESE YAO DONG

Some forty million Chinese live in subterranean dwellings or in terraces of earth-roof caves, known collectively as *yao dong* or simply *yao* (which means "kiln"; *dong* means "cave"). These are dug into the world's largest "dissected plateau," which is covered to a depth of up to 656 feet (200 m) by finely textured silts (*loess*) that have blown in over the centuries from the Gobi Desert and Mongolia.

Within China, these ocher-colored uplands stretch in a band from the provinces of Henan and Shanxi in the north to Shaanxi and Gansu in the northwest. Trees are scarce, so wood is at a premium. This arid region has little rainfall and endures extreme temperatures—in summer, above 95° F (35° C); in winter, below freezing. In response to these conditions, throughout much of this region at least twenty percent of the rural population live in yao dong; in northern Shaanxi, this rises to fifty and even eighty percent.

They are two main types of yao dong—those that are built into a cliffside (also known as *dishang*) and pit-type yao dong with sunken courtyards. Although these are commonly called cave dwellings, they are entirely man-made, earth-sheltered environments, which, says Chinese vernacular expert Ronald G. Knapp, "acquire a singular identity from their internal form instead of their external design." In the case of cliffside dwellings, the earth removed to create them is used to level the site or build earthen walls to create courtyards.

These earth-sheltered dwellings provide protection from a hostile environment. They are cool in summer and warm in winter, but have limited interior light, high humidity levels, and inadequate ventilation—problems the Chinese government is trying to address by building modern forms of yao dong in accordance with sustainable design principles. One problem that is harder to solve is that a yao dong is a dangerous place to be in during an earthquake, which are periodic in the loessial uplands. In 1921, more than a million people died in collapsing yao dong in a single quake.

SEE ALSO

> Mediterranean Cave Dwellings, pages 72–73

> Cappadocian Cave Dwellings, pages 74–75

This "dissected plateau" is an area that has been uplifted and then severely eroded so that the relief is sharp and mountainous.

HENAN,SHANXI, SHAANXI,GANSU PROVINCES,CHINA

MATERIALS

* Caves or pits dug out of loess (finely textured silt)

* Brick for front walls

PIT COURTYARD DWELLINGS

"Pit courtyard" subterranean dwellings are usually square. Two or three yao dong are dug into the vertical side walls of the courtyard, which are sometimes faced with brick. A ramp or stairs provides access from ground level. Trees are often planted in the courtyard, which serves as a family or community space.

CLIFFSIDE DWELLINGS

Cliffside dwellings are dug horizontally into the slopes of hills or the sides of ravines. They face south, thus benefiting from the winter sun. If the slope has stable soil and good drainage, several terraces of such dwellings may well be built at staggered intervals.

CLIFFSIDE DWELLING CROSS SECTION

This diagram of the internal structure of a typical cliff cave dwelling shows eight rectangular rooms, radiating off a central space. The rooms are limited to a maximum width of 12 feet (3.5 m) due to constraints imposed by the stability of the soil, and to a maximum length by the penetration of sunlight. These factors determine the room's furniture arrangements (pictured right).

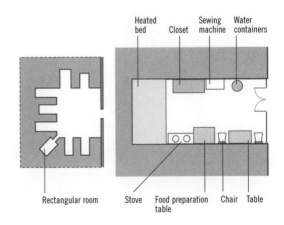

Rectangular room

Heated bed   Closet   Sewing machine   Water containers

Stove   Food preparation table   Chair   Table

FROM JAPANESE MINKA TO TODA HUTS
FUJIAN TULOU

The mountainous areas of western Fujian province in southwest China are home to a unique form of rammed-earth building known as a *tulou*—large defensive structures designed to contain and protect one family clan. UNESCO has estimated that twenty thousand tulou survive on forty-six main sites; a thousand of these are *yanlou* (round buildings), which can exceed 33 feet (10 m) in height and 197 feet (60 m) in diameter.

Tulou were built from the thirteenth to the twentieth centuries by the Hakka and southern Fujian people to protect themselves from armed bandits. These enclosed fortlike buildings, which could take seven years to build, have rounded stone foundations and a base of large stones, plastered with clay, which support 6-foot (1.8-m)-thick earth walls, reinforced by bamboo canes. The building's interior is a largely wood structure of beams, decks, and columns, which contains 250 small uniform dwelling units, housing some eighty families. These face a central communal courtyard, in which an ancestral shrine provides a focus for the entire community. Only one side gets direct sunlight. The mud-wall facade is largely blank, with small windows on the upper floors protected by the large, overhanging eaves of the cantilevered slate or clay-tile roof. There is usually one main entrance, heavily guarded by a thick armor-plate wood door set in a solid block of granite.

On the ground floor are the communal kitchens, with grain stores above them, and rooms used for eating and washing. Steep stairs lead up to the first and second floors, which house the living and sleeping quarters and have verandas. Food, clothing, and valuables are stored on the third floor. A small family owns a vertical "set" of these rooms; a larger family might own two or three. Tulou were constructed up until the 1960s; fortified buildings are now illegal in China. A number are still inhabited, but many tulou clans have been split up by the state and now live in separate family units.

SEE ALSO

> Batammaliba Roundhouse, pages 110–11

> Lhasa Buildings, pages 96–97

MATERIALS

* Stone for foundations and base of walls, later plastered with clay

* Rammed earth for thick walls, reinforced by bamboo canes

* Wood for internal framework of beams, decks, and columns

* Slate or clay tiles for roof

Fujian province is traditionally described as eight parts mountain, one part water, and one part farmland.

FUJIAN
PROVINCE,
CHINA

CROSS SECTION

This isometric view of a circular tulou gives a clear view of the many aspects and levels of these complex structures, the only circular buildings known in China. The circular form has several practical advantages, being easier to build and more economic in the use of materials. It also has greater stability.

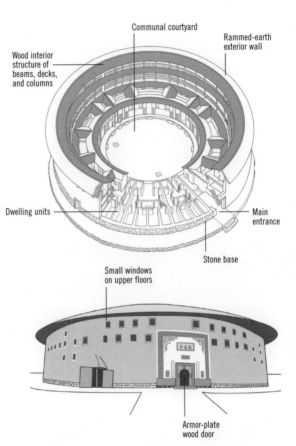

Communal courtyard

Rammed-earth exterior wall

Wood interior structure of beams, decks, and columns

Dwelling units

Main entrance

Stone base

KING OF TULOUS

The most famous Chinese tulou is Chengqilou, built in 1709, a massive rotunda with four concentric rings, with an ancestral hall in the center, which was used to house eighty families. The most significant feature of this huge collective dwelling is the fact that all its residents had an equal share of the living spaces. The outer ring is 205 feet (62.6 m) in diameter, and has two main gates and two side gates.

Small windows on upper floors

Armor-plate wood door

CONCENTRIC CIRCLES

This internal view of Chengqilou shows the four concentric-ring structure of this extraordinary building. Going outward from the center, we see the ancestral hall surrounded by a circular covered corridor. The second ring is one story high, has thirty-two rooms, and served as a community library. The third ring is two stories high, with forty rooms on each level. The outer ring is four stories high, with seventy-two rooms on each level—a total of four hundred rooms.

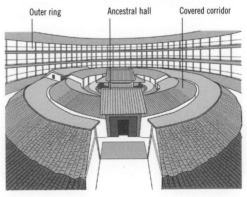

Outer ring

Ancestral hall

Covered corridor

MONGOLIAN GER

The *ger*—the equivalent of the Turkish *yurt*—is the traditional shelter of the herding peoples of the high Mongolian steppes, seemingly endless expanses of grass-covered land that cover the majority of eastern Mongolia and extend in a narrow band to the west, sandwiched between high mountains to the north and west and the Gobi Desert to the south. These vast open grasslands are grazed by an estimated population of thirty million sheep, goats, cows, and camels, owned by seminomadic herders, who make up thirty percent of the country's 2.9 million people. The ger (which means "home" in Mongolian) is ideally suited to the herders' lifestyle as they follow their animals in search of fresh pasture on a regular or seasonal basis.

For a start, it is easy to erect, dismantle and transport; it takes no more than an hour to pack a ger and a family's belongings inside a truck or onto a train of horses, yaks, or camels. Gers are also well suited to the climate, which consists of long cold winters, when temperatures can drop to –22° F (–30° C), and short, hot, and rainy summers. In winter, the gers are heated by simple stoves, and extra layers of felt can be added for warmth; in the summer, the bottom of the covers can be turned up for extra ventilation. These felt-lined tents are a herder's most important possession. A ger accommodates the whole family and also serves as a sacred space, where the orientation and interior layout have profound symbolic significance.

In modern times, the materials used for constructing gers have changed. Canvas is now frequently used to provide an extra layer for protection from the rain. In addition, a white cotton cover is now commonplace, whereas previously this was only used on the gers of nobles. Vast numbers of Mongolians have moved to the cities where most live in apartment buildings; many others have created ger cities, informal settlements where families live in small wood houses alongside their cherished gers.

SEE ALSO

> Rendille Min, pages 112–13

> Plains Indian Tipi, pages 126–27

> Sami Gamme and Goatte, pages 48–49

MONGOLIA

Mongolia is a landlocked country, slightly smaller than Alaska, situated in a strategic location between China and Russia. It is the most sparsely populated country in the world.

MATERIALS

* Felt, made from sheep's wool

* Ropes, made from horse or camel hair

* Wood poles, lattice, and door frame

BUILDING THE GER

The concertina lattice panels, usually made from flexible willow, are expanded and tied together to form the basic circular structure; a band of webbing holds them firm, and the solid, wood door frame helps to stabilize the ger. The roof compression ring and crown are erected in the center, and the curved roof pole is then fitted into place.

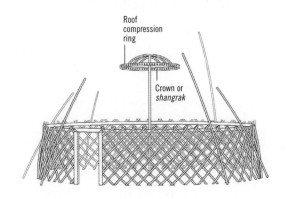

Roof compression ring

Crown or *shangrak*

ROOF AND COVERING

The felt mats are tied on with ropes woven from animal hair or made from thin strips of hide. The felt is thick, made from sheep's wool, and waterproofed by rubbing it with animal fat and lanolin. The door always faces south—traditionally, it's believed that the spirit of the home lives in the threshold. The compression ring, which enables the smoke to escape, is known as the shangrak, and may be passed down through families. Even if a ger is completely repaired or replaced, the shangrak is generally retained.

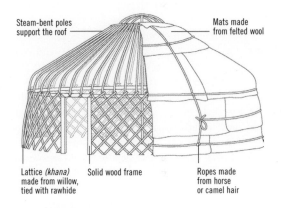

Steam-bent poles support the roof

Mats made from felted wool

Lattice *(khana)* made from willow, tied with rawhide

Solid wood frame

Ropes made from horse or camel hair

INSIDE THE GER

Traditionally, space is allocated according to Mongolian rules of etiquette, with prescribed places for men, women, guests, household objects, cooking, living, and sleeping. Everything centers on the fire, which is sometimes set in a square hearth. Gers are pitched facing south, so that as the sun moves across the sky, it shines down through the shangrak, creating a form of indoor sundial.

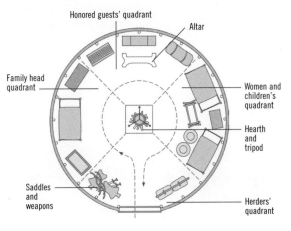

Honored guests' quadrant

Altar

Family head quadrant

Women and children's quadrant

Hearth and tripod

Saddles and weapons

Herders' quadrant

LHASA BUILDINGS

Vernacular buildings around the world are threatened by modern development, and this is the case in Lhasa, the Tibetan capital, which has been subject to widespread modernization in recent years by the Chinese government. In a model project, the Tibetan Heritage Fund (THF) set out to record and conserve the city's traditional architecture. "The Old Town Conservation Project," which ran from 1996 to 2000, identified ninety-three historical buildings in the Barkor district of the city, creating a detailed database and map in the process. As a result, these buildings gained protection by the Lhasa authorities and work began on their conservation.

Three hundred Tibetans were trained to work on the project; some in traditional building skills, others as surveyors, plumbers, electricians, and project managers. Only fifty out of the ninety-three historical residential buildings in the district were saved, but the inner Barkor neighborhood has been conserved and is today still inhabited by its original community. The UN Human Settlement Program awarded the project "best practice" status in 2004.

The buildings pictured opposite represent three forms of the Tibetan vernacular: a typical Tibetan temple; a "noble house" (*zim-sha*), an opulent building with bay windows and carved decoration of much higher quality than an ordinary Tibetan dwelling; a community courtyard building. The temple style was particularly influential. According to the THF, "For nearly a millennium, Tibetan architecture was the preferred medium for construction of monasteries and palaces across much of Inner Asia, including northern India and Pakistan, Bhutan and Nepal, northern China, Mongolia, and parts of Siberia." The ground floor contains a main chapel (circled by a corridor that pilgrims would pace), in front of which is a large assembly hall for the monks, in turn fronted by an entrance porch with stairs to the second floor, where a small chapel and room used by the head monk are located.

SEE ALSO

> Balinese Kuren,
  pages 154–55

> Yemen Tower House,
  pages 78–79

> Fujian Tulou,
  pages 92–93

MATERIALS

* Lumber for wood structure of pillars, capitals, and beams and rafters

* Earth for constructing walls and roof

* Clay tiles for roof

The Tibetan plateau—"the roof of the world"—covers 965 square miles (2.5 million sq km), about four times the size of France.

LHASA REGION, TIBET

TYPICAL TEMPLE

The basic Tibetan form is a two-story structure made of tapering earth walls with an internal wood structure of pillars, capitals, and beams. The earth roof is supported by wood rafters, covered with scraps of wood, branches, and twigs to close any gaps in the structure, and finished off with a layer of rounded pebbles on which is laid a thick layer of earth. The second-floor structures are topped with pitched, tiled roofs.

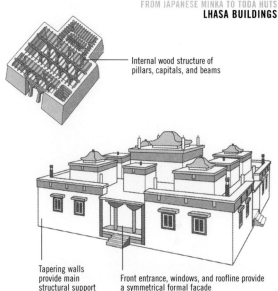

Internal wood structure of pillars, capitals, and beams

Tapering walls provide main structural support

Front entrance, windows, and roofline provide a symmetrical formal facade

NOBLE HOUSE

This cross section shows the three-story living quarters on the left, adjacent to a two-story outbuilding that contains stables on the ground floor and servants' quarters above, with a main gate leading through a courtyard to the main building. This contains store rooms on the ground floor, living quarters for house servants, and a family chapel on the middle floor, with living quarters for the family of the owner.

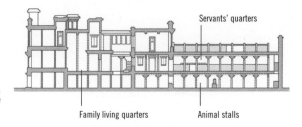

Servants' quarters

Family living quarters

Animal stalls

GO-RA DWELLING

The ground plan of a *go-ra* ("ordinary dwelling"), a simple and functional building, two or three stories high, consisted of numerous tenanted dwellings around a central courtyard, a form that evolved from the traditional caravansery, built to house some of the large floating population of traders that visited Lhasa. These buildings were often owned by monasteries, and operated to generate income from up to fifty tenants.

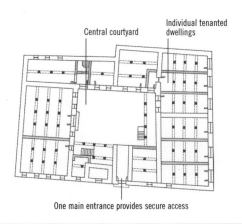

Central courtyard

Individual tenanted dwellings

One main entrance provides secure access

INDIAN STEPPED PONDS AND STEPWELLS

SEE ALSO

> Cappadocian
Cave Dwellings,
pages 74–75

> Iranian Desert
Towns, pages 82–83

Modern India is beginning to rediscover the stepped ponds and stepwells that form an important part of the historical vernacular architecture of western India. At present, says author Marco Beach, "these are the least known or visited monuments in India." He says they are also "among the greatest examples of ecologically sensitive architecture in any country." For fourteen centuries, they provided access to groundwater and collected the rainwater from the monsoons—which last for just twelve weeks—and held it through the dry months of the year. Apart from a few in Delhi, all surviving early examples can be found in the desert states of Gujarat and Rajasthan, where thousands were built in villages and cities.

The stepwells are subterranean water reservoirs, housed in highly decorated linear stone temples, in which numerous flights of stairs, with columned pavilions on each landing, lead many levels downward to a water pool deep below. Designed by masons and built with the labor of the people, they were funded by royal families or rich merchants as monuments to their generosity to the whole community. Here people could drink, wash, and bathe, or simply sit at any level in the coolness, socializing or contemplating the beauty of their surroundings. They became an integral part of community life, and were also the scene of special festivals and sacred rites.

Stepped ponds are usually square, are always found near a temple, and were used solely for bathing and rituals. The Hindus believe that purification with water is an essential aspect of everyday spiritual life and thus a daily bath cleanses your sins and is the moment when one is closest to heaven. The four walls of a stepped pond, according to author Morna Livingston, "are made of short flights of stairs that meet at small landings. It has no columns or covered spaces.... Taken as a whole, the building is like one giant folding stair, which, like origami, has no form separate from its surface."

The Thar desert, also known as the Great Indian Desert, covers an area of approximately 77,000 square miles (200,000 sq km) in five Indian states.

**RAJASTHAN
STATE, INDIA**

MATERIALS

* Stone for flights
of stairs, columned
pavilions, and lining
the water pool

STEPWELL

Stepwells are triumphs of architecture and engineering and come in a wide variety of styles and sizes, from the monumental to the modest. In this view, you can see the entrance gate and the beginning of the long flight of steps of a stepwell, with colonnades on either side, which goes down five levels into the earth.

PLAN AND CROSS SECTION

This plan and cross section of a stepwell show how the stepped corridor is punctuated by numerous intermediate, towerlike pavilions. One way of visualizing it is as a giant triangular wedge, with a horizontal line running at ground level, a vertical plunging into the earth, and a long diagonal marking the line of the steps.

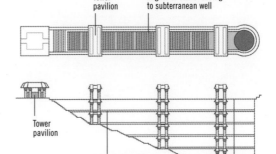

Tower pavilion

Flights of stairs leading to subterranean well

Tower pavilion

Narrow platforms link pavilions

STEPPED POND

Stepped ponds were easier to construct than stepwells, and were less polluted. The square stepped pond creates a powerful visual effect, like an M. C. Escher drawing, composed as it is of a zigzag of stairs, each flight of which is half a matched pair, placed back-to-back to form a triangle. Like chanting a mantra, the process of choosing a pathway and following it step by step to the bathing pool below held spiritual significance.

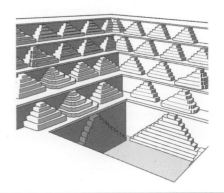

TODA HUT

The Toda tribe, who live in the Nilgiri plateau of southern India, number fewer than a thousand people and thus represent what anthropological linguist M. B. Emeneau called "a minuscule fragment of the great Indian population." However, they have been extensively studied by Western ethnographers, musicologists, and other scholars who have shown intense interest in their religious rituals, social organization, language, origins, and appearance, their preeminent art form—extempore (improvised) singing—and their architecture.

"Toda traditional houses are marvels of tribal architecture," writes conservationist and photographer Tarun Chabra. "These can last for many decades, only requiring periodic rethatching, in areas where the annual precipitation can reach 157 inches (4,000 mm). Even when it is bitterly cold or windy outside, these are very warm within.... Despite having hardly any foundation, they act as natural wind-breakers and remain intact even after the most violent storm. They also blend superbly with the undulating terrain." A traditional Toda village *(mund)* would consist of up to ten of these huts but, by the early 1990s, there were only half a dozen of these barrel-vault homes left standing in total, because most of the Toda were living in modern mud and concrete housing. However, Chabra and his colleagues have, in the last ten years or so, managed to get government and private funding to build more than forty new traditional houses.

Other changes are also threatening Toda culture. Each village used to own a herd of a special breed of water buffalo, which required no shelter and lived on the coarse grass of the high plateau. These animals not only provided the tribe's basic income, through selling dairy products to their neighbors, but some were also considered sacred. Many villages had conical dairy temples, administered by a dairyman-priest. The spread of modern agricultural methods has greatly diminished the buffalo herds, and international efforts are now under way to save both the people and their environment.

SEE ALSO

> Abelam Spirit House pages 162–63

> Kalinga Octagonal House, pages 156–57

MATERIALS

* Thick poles to create structure ` of curved, arched roof, secured with rattan ropes

* Wood or granite stones to support structure at either end

* Swamp grass for thatch

The Nilgiri Biosphere Reserve has been established to help preserve the Toda culture.

NILGIRI
PLATEAU, INDIA

FRAMEWORK

The traditional houses of the
Toda tribe are rectangular half-
barrel-shape huts, the main
structural element of which is
a curved, arched roof of thick
bamboo poles—the thickest
forming the ridge—supported
at each end by either dressed
granite stones or wood planks
(pictured). These are secured
using multiple lengths of rattan.

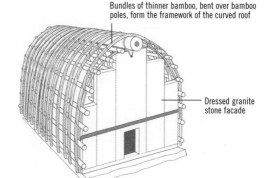

Bundles of thinner bamboo, bent over bamboo
poles, form the framework of the curved roof

Dressed granite
stone facade

BAMBOO ROOF

The framework is overlain by a
dense covering of thinner bamboo
canes running horizontally along
the length of the hut, likewise
fastened with rattan ropes.
The average Toda hut measures
10 feet (3 m) high, 18 feet (5.5 m)
long, and 9 feet (2.7 m) wide.

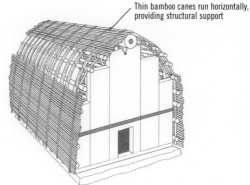

Thin bamboo canes run horizontally,
providing structural support

FINISHED HUT

The completed roof is then
elaborately thatched with dried
swamp grass and the front and
back of the hut are decorated
with paintings. The structure has
no windows and a tiny entrance
at the front—no more than
3 feet (90 cm) wide and 3 feet
(90 cm) tall—which provides
protection against wild animals.
The hut itself is surrounded by a
wall of loose stones.

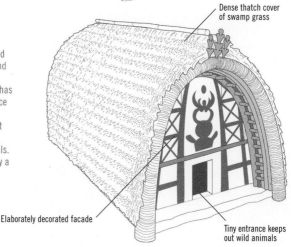

Dense thatch cover
of swamp grass

Elaborately decorated facade

Tiny entrance keeps
out wild animals

FROM ZULU INDLU TO
THE "VENICE OF AFRICA"

One of the most impressive buildings in the whole of Africa, the Great Mosque of Djenné, symbolizes and celebrates the innovative earth architecture of Mali. The distinctive toleks of the Mousgoum people and the Batammaliba roundhouses display similar qualities on a human scale. Stilt dwellings are the only housing solution for the people of Ganvié, dubbed the "Venice of Africa." The Rendille herders shelter in whelk-shaped tents, while the Zafimaniry people of Madagascar build houses from bamboo and wood that evolve into a more permanent form as the relationship of its married owners deepens. In the south, the Zulu's beehive indlus and the painted houses of the Ndebele are widely celebrated as expressions of their differing, but equally vibrant, cultures.

GREAT MOSQUE OF DJENNE

The Great Mosque of Djenné in Mali, a country famous for its earth architecture, is the largest mud-brick building in the world and one of the most famous landmarks in Africa. Along with the old town of Djenné, it was designated a World Heritage Site by UNESCO in 1988. Djenné was a flourishing center on the Trans-Saharan trade network, and it was Arab traders who first introduced Islam, leading to the building of the first mosque on the site in the thirteenth century. This was demolished in 1834, rebuilt in 1896, then demolished again to make way for the current structure, which was completed in 1907, during the French administration.

The Great Mosque is built on a raised platform, with a surface area of 62,500 square feet (5,625 sq m), to protect it from the annual flooding of the Bani River, which turns Djenné into an island and can flood parts of the city. This has so far protected the mosque from even the most severe floods. The prayer wall *(quibla)*, which faces east toward Mecca, is supported by eighteen buttresses and is punctuated by three large boxlike minarets, each of which contains a spiral staircase leading to the roof and is capped by a cone-shape spire crowned with an ostrich egg. Half of the mosque forms an interior prayer hall, covered by a roof supported by ninety wood pillars, which can hold three thousand people. Behind this is an open-air prayer hall in the form of a courtyard, which is enclosed on three sides by walls punctuated with arched openings, and on the fourth by the mosque itself.

For many years, a spring festival *(crepissage),* supervised by a guild of eighty senior masons, has been staged at which the entire community of Djenné takes part in replastering the mosque to repair any weather damage that may have occurred during the past twelve months. The spring festival now also involves foreign visitors, as tourism provides the majority of income for Djenné.

MALI

The landlocked nation of Mali is one of the poorest nations in the world, and is comparable in size to South Africa. Most of the country lies in the southern Sahara.

SEE ALSO

> New Mexican Adobe House, pages 136–37

MATERIALS

* Sun-baked mud bricks, coated with mud plaster to form the walls

* Palm branches, which are built into the structure

* Ceramic pipes to provide drainage

* Ostrich eggs for the minarets

MOSQUE WALLS

The huge walls of the Great Mosque, which are 16–24 inches (41–61 cm) thick, depending on their height, are made of sun-baked mud bricks *(ferey)* coated with a mud plaster, which gives the building its smooth, sculpted look. They keep the building cool during the day and gradually release the heat they have absorbed at night, which keeps the mosque warm.

PROTECTIVE STRUCTURE

The facade of the mosque has the same structure and building materials as a traditional house in Djenné. Although it has many architectural elements similar to mosques throughout the Islamic world, the use of local materials and traditional styles makes it uniquely African. To protect the building from the local climate, with its frequent and drastic changes in humidity and temperature, palm branches have been built into the structure to reduce cracking and to serve as ready-made scaffolding for annual repairs. Gutters made of ceramic pipes also stick out from the structure to direct water draining from the roof away from the walls. The ostrich eggs, which symbolize purity and fertility, symbolically protect the highest and most vulnerable tips of the minarets.

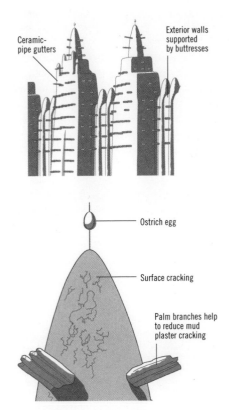

Ceramic-pipe gutters

Exterior walls supported by buttresses

Ostrich egg

Surface cracking

Palm branches help to reduce mud plaster cracking

MOUSGOUM TOLEK

Among the most extraordinary of all African vernacular structures are the celebrated bullet-shaped earth houses known as *toleks*. Built by the Mousgoum people, who live on either side of the Logone River, which divides northern Cameroon and Chad, these unique mud huts have no supporting structure, because wood is a scarce resource. André Gide saw them in 1925 and famously celebrated them in his travel journals: "The [Mousgoum's] hut . . . resembles no other; but it is not strange, it is beautiful; and it is not its strangeness so much as its beauty that moves me . . . this hut is made by hand like a vase; it is the work, not of a mason, but of a potter. Its color is the very color of the earth—a pinkish-gray clay."

Built without foundations on a mound of flattened earth, the entire structure is made of a progression of circular walls, 16–23 feet (5–7 m) in diameter, constructed of balls of clay mixed with straw and smoothed by hand, that lean slightly inward and get gradually narrower as they reach the top, forming a parabolic shape. The outside is covered with protruding ribs, which add to the structural stability, but also offer footholds to make it easy to climb up and thus to build it without the aid of scaffolding. A circular opening at the top serves as a skylight and chimney. The difference in height between the door and the top—a completed hut is 23–26 feet (7–8 m) high—ensures there is a natural draft to carry the smoke upward.

According to Steven Nelson, in his book *From Cameroon to Paris: Mousgoum In and Out of Africa*, toleks (pl. *tolekakay*) started to die out in the 1930s and few were left standing by the 1990s. However, he reports that, since 1955, there has been a resurgence in the building of toleks, and as a result some twenty new ones have been built. There has also been what he calls a "virtual explosion" in wall painting, much of which depicts the distinctive form of the tolek.

SEE ALSO
> Cob House,
  pages 54–55
> Trullo Stone House,
  pages 70–71
> Inuit Igloo,
  pages 122–23

CHAD/CAMEROON

Cameroon is often described as "Africa in miniature," as it experiences all of Africa's major climates and can support most of the continent's vegetation. It is home to some three hundred different ethnic and linguistic groups.

MATERIALS

* Balls of clay, mixed with straw, arranged in layers, to build the main structure on a mound of flattened earth

CLASSIC TOLEK

The classic shape of the Mousgoum tolek has been much admired by Western artists and architects for its handmade grace and practicality. The distinctive protruding ribs aid construction without scaffolding; the keyhole entrance enables cattle, sheep, and goats to enter the hut at night. They sleep behind a low wall that rings the inside of the hut.

TOLEK COMPOUND

The Mousgoum's "house" is composed of a number of toleks set around the edge of a circular courtyard, all linked together by a low earthen wall. The entrance to the compound is located between the man's two toleks; the woman has a bedroom and a kitchen, the latter being built on a smaller scale.

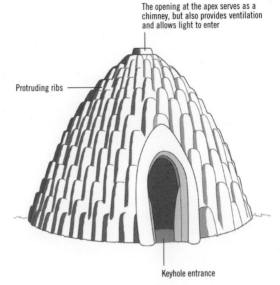

The opening at the apex serves as a chimney, but also provides ventilation and allows light to enter

Protruding ribs

Keyhole entrance

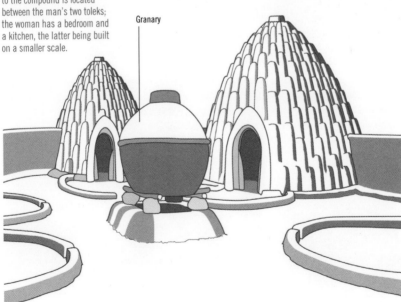

Granary

GANVIE STILT VILLAGE

Often referred to as the "Venice of West Africa," the town of Ganvié on Lake Nokoué in Benin (formerly Dahomey)— a huge brackish lake fed by the major north–south rivers—is the biggest lake-dwelling stilt town in Africa, with some three thousand houses and a population of twenty-five thousand inhabitants. The town was first established at the end of the seventeenth century, at a time when the armies of the kings of Dahomey were raiding villages to capture the inhabitants to sell as slaves to the Portuguese, a practice that continued until the end of the nineteenth century and provided abundant slaves for the Americas. In order to avoid capture, the Tofinu people escaped first to the lake and its surrounding marshlands, where they established Ganvié, a name that means "safe at last."

The Ganviéns of today make a living by fishing and trading at a daily floating market, conducted from numerous wood boats known as *pirogues,* which also provide transport from the mainland. The whole life of the town is conducted on and in the water. There are some small artificial islands in Ganvié on which a school, a cemetery, and other social facilities are situated.

The main activity of the men of Ganvié is fishing with a round net from a pirogue. They also make large net traps from a maze of branches planted in the mud, from which the fish cannot escape once they enter. Here the fish develop and grow and are harvested periodically. Women dry and smoke the fish and sell them on the market. They also fetch and sell drinking water, because the waters of the lake have become increasingly saline since the creation of a channel linking the lake to the sea in the 1880s.

In modern times, there has been a drastic drop in the fishermen's catch, an increase in water pollution, and a rise in the infant mortality rate. Ganvié has also become a significant tourist destination.

SEE ALSO

> Paisa House,
  pages 146–47

> Korowai Tree House,
  pages 160–61

> Samoan Fale Tele,
  pages 168–69

> Aboriginal Shelter
  (Platform Shelter),
  pages 164–65

BENIN

The long, narrow country of Benin extends inland for 400 miles (650 km), but is only 200 miles (325 km) across at its widest point. It has a hot, humid climate, with two rainy and two dry seasons a year.

MATERIALS

* Mangrove poles to make the stilt frame

* Wood to make the floors and walls

* Palm fronds and grass thatch, or corrugated iron, for the roof

RECTANGULAR STILT HOUSE

A typical rectangular plan house in Ganvié is, according to author Paul Oliver, built on a stilt frame of mangrove poles with floors raised above flood level. They have hipped or gabled roofs, which are first covered with palm fronds that are then overlaid with a thick grass thatch. Most of the houses do not have electricity, so people use either kerosene or solar power and cook on an open fire.

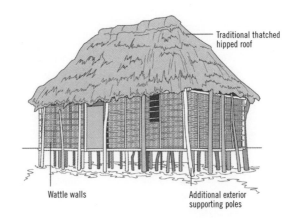

Traditional thatched hipped roof

Wattle walls

Additional exterior supporting poles

GANVIÉ CAFÉ

This unusual example of vernacular building is the "Cité Lacustre Ganvié Café." It is painted a garish pink, has many gables topped by spear-shaped finials, and incorporates modern materials. Its wide veranda caters not only to the community, but also to the increasing number of tourists who come to see this unique lakeland settlement.

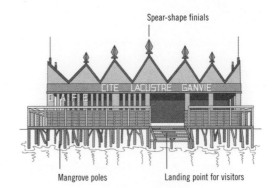

Spear-shape finials

Mangrove poles

Landing point for visitors

STILT HOUSE AT WATER LEVEL

At flood time, the Ganvié houses' stiltlike legs disappear beneath the waters, leaving the main house structure sitting on the surface. The level of the floors in a Ganvié house are determined by the water level at high flooding and are usually 5 feet (1.5 m) above low water.

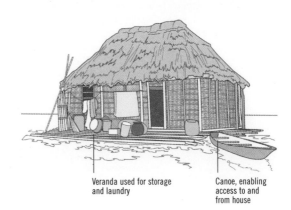

Veranda used for storage and laundry

Canoe, enabling access to and from house

FROM ZULU INDLU TO THE "VENICE OF AFRICA"
BATAMMALIBA ROUNDHOUSE

The Batammaliba people, who live in the northern regions of Togo and Benin, West Africa, have long been recognized as among the greatest vernacular architects of Africa. Their name means "those who are the real architects of the earth," reflecting the importance of architecture within their culture. The Western traveller Leo Frobenius encountered them in 1913 and called their remarkable two-story earth houses "artworks," describing them "genuinely and rightly as small castles." According to Suzanne Preston Blier, who lived with the Batammaliba and wrote a definitive study of them, each roundhouse functions as a self-sufficient economic unit—incorporating special areas for sheltering animals, drying crops, preparing food, and storing grain. Each house is surrounded by an area of land, fertilized by the animals, and used for growing crops.

The single most important figure in the community is the earth priest, who is responsible for the village and its architecture. Also revered are the architects *(otammali),* who are involved in building the houses, aided by the house owner and his family. Each ottomali's design has to be approved by a group of community master architects. House construction is generally undertaken in the dry season (from December to February) and each architect builds one house per season. Each house is built in courses, one layer per day, beginning with the main rooms and the outer joining walls. When complete, the women cover the terrace and exterior walls with a plaster made of silt, fruit essence, dung, and oil to protect the earthen core from rain. While the plaster is still wet, they draw patterns in it with their fingers. When dry, they stain the walls with a fruit juice and water solution that produces a deep maroon or brown finish.

Each part of the building has great significance, relating both to different organs of the body and to spiritual and cosmological beliefs.

SEE ALSO

> Fujian Tulou, pages 92–93

> Ndebele Painted House, pages 118–19

The Batammaliba people live on fertile plains dominated by the Ataccora Mountains. They are believed to have arrived there in the seventeenth or eighteenth century.

TOGO/BENIN

MATERIALS

* Earth, to build ring of seven earthen towers

* Thatch to top towers

* Wood frameworks to support roof terrace

ROUNDHOUSE PLAN

The basic form of the Batammaliba house is a ring of seven earthen towers, linked together by semicircular walls to form a seamless protective outer shell. Inside the ring there is another circular thatched tower in the center, which is surrounded by an earthen roof terrace, supported underneath by a wood framework, which extends to the outer ring. Important elements of the building contain altars and shrines; the whole village is also mapped out with a network of ritual paths, which relate to the image of Butan, the female earth goddess.

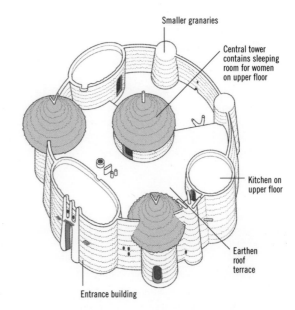

Smaller granaries

Central tower contains sleeping room for women on upper floor

Kitchen on upper floor

Earthen roof terrace

Entrance building

ROUNDHOUSE FACADE

In the center of the facade of the house is a west-facing doorway, above which are two or three earthen "entry horns." On each corner of the facade are two thatched granaries (one male, one female), each supported by a tall earthen tower, which have shelters for chickens or ducks in their base. The oval entrance building is where crops, such as millet and sorghum, are ground; the chamber above holds a sleeping compartment. Behind the granaries are two towers with flat earth roofs, both of which have ground-floor storage rooms. One houses the main kitchen on the upper floor. Two smaller granary structures complete the outer ring. The central tower has a sleeping room for the women on the upper floor.

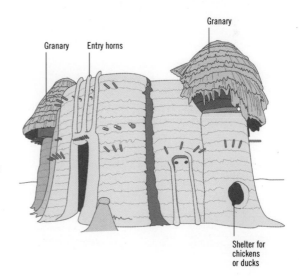

Granary

Entry horns

Granary

Shelter for chickens or ducks

RENDILLE MIN

The Rendille camel nomads live on semiarid lowlands in northern Kenya, in light, portable shelters they call *min*. Shaped like a whelk's shell, the min's physical structure is highly practical. The back half, which is tall enough to stand up in, is the sleeping area. The back wall is covered with hides to keep out the wind at night. Personal possessions are hung from the roof. The wider, more open front half of the min is the public area, where firewood, sandals, and milking vessels are stored.

On average, a Rendille settlement would consist of thirty to fifty mins, which would be moved six times a year in search of fresh pastures and water, or to escape from conflict. Each married woman or widow owns a min, which is built for her on the day of her marriage; from then on, she is responsible for it. On the day of a move, the women rise before dawn, dismantle the mins, and load them on camels. The long arched main frames are tied vertically to the sides of the camel and held together at the top. In the space between are stacked the shorter sticks and rolls of roof and floor mats, topped by a cone of wall and floor skins. In front are large containers and the clay cooking pot in its basket.

Within three hours, the settlement is on the move and will travel distances of 25 miles (40 km) in a day. Before the sun sets, the women unload the camels and rebuild the houses, and the men fence the animals. Anders Grum, a Danish architect and anthropologist, traced the movement of one nomadic group in detail and calculated that, over a seventy-year period, they traveled approximately 12,000 miles (19,000 km). However, in more recent times, many Rendille settlements have stabilized near townships and become dependent on them; they have also become separated from regular contact with their livestock, which are now looked after in smaller, more mobile camps.

SEE ALSO

> Sami Gamme and Goatte, pages 48–49

> Mongolian Ger, pages 94–95

> Plains Indian Tipi, pages 126–27

> Aboriginal Shelter, pages 164–65

> Abelam Spirit House, pages 162–63

MATERIALS

* Wood poles and sticks to define the basic frame

* Sisal tiles, overlapped and tied to the structure, to provide a covering

* Cowhides, to frame the entrance and provide a windbreak at the rear of the shelter

The camel is essential to the Rendille, providing them with transportation and their staple food, known as banjo, *which consists of camel meat and a mixture of milk and blood.*

KENYA

MIN FRAME

The basic frame of a min consists of two main parts, the curved back and the fanlike front. The back is defined by two pairs of long curved poles, one of which provides the leading edge, the other a curved brace to the rear. Thinner sticks are lashed to these to form the domed sleeping quarters. The front consists of a fan of straight sticks, inclined inward, spaced at regular intervals and secured by stones.

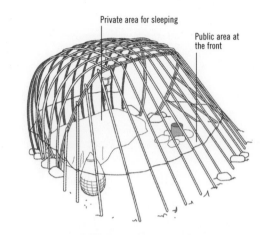

Private area for sleeping

Public area at the front

MIN SIDE VIEW

This view of the min shows that the rear section allows for standing room. Stones are used to help position the curved frame on the ground. The wider front section of the min is a public area and is without floor coverings.

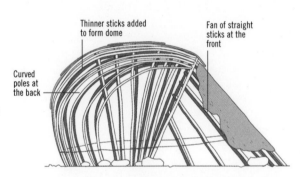

Thinner sticks added to form dome

Fan of straight sticks at the front

Curved poles at the back

COVERING

When the skeleton of the min is complete, it is covered with "tiles" made of sisal, a stiff, long-lasting plant fiber, which are overlapped and tied to the structure. A long rope is bound around the whole min to provide further stability.

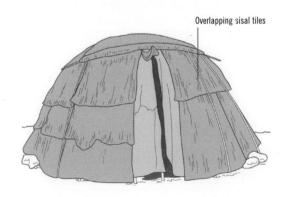

Overlapping sisal tiles

ZAFIMANIRY HOUSE

To the Zafimaniry people of Madagascar, wood plays a central role in all aspects of life and death, and the structure and building of their decorative wood houses carry important social and symbolic significance. Some twenty-five thousand Zafimaniry live in about one hundred villages and hamlets scattered in the wooded highlands of southeast Madagascar. The men living in this unique community are foresters, carpenters, and craft workers of great knowledge and skill, who not only build houses and tombs in wood but also create a wide variety of everyday objects, such as rosewood chairs, stools, honey pots, and chests that they sell to make a living.

All are highly decorated with geometric patterns that carry rich symbolic significance and traces of both their Polynesian origins and the Arabic influences on Malagasy culture. The wood they use comes from twenty different species of local trees, each of which is employed for a specific type of construction or decorative function.

To the Zafimaniry, building a house and making a marriage are two sides of a single process. When a young couple tell their parents of their intentions, the man builds a flimsy and fragile house out of soft, permeable bamboo. As the relationship strengthens, the bamboo is replaced with hardwood planks, a process they call "acquiring bones." Over time, the house becomes an entirely wooden structure, decorated throughout, and develops into a "holy house" that will be passed on to the couple's descendants.

Zafimaniry culture is now endangered. Despite the demand for their work, little of the money comes to the makers, and counterfeiting is rife. In addition, the deforestation of the region, made worse by slash-and-burn agriculture, means that their raw material is running short. Younger people, rather than training in traditional woodcrafts, are leaving to find work in the towns. A UNESCO action plan is trying both to protect the natural environment of the Zafimaniry and to preserve their traditional techniques.

SEE ALSO

> Russian Izba,
   pages 62–63

> Shaker-Style
   Buildings,
   pages 134–35

> Caribbean
   Chattel House,
   pages 142–43

MATERIALS

* Woven bamboo to make the first form of the house

* Long, flattened bamboo stalks for roofing

* Hardwood planks to make the wall of the finished house

Much of the natural habitat of Madagascar is being destroyed, despite the fact that it is a jewel of biodiversity. Some five percent of the world's species live here, including eight thousand species of flowering plants alone.

MADAGASCAR

TYPICAL HOUSE

A typical Zafimaniry one-room house, initially built out of woven bamboo, gradually acquires "bones" as the bamboo is replaced by large wooden hardwood planks, assembled using mortise-and-tenon joints and wood pegs, without any nails or metal hinges. This vernacular style is classified as Neo-Indonesian.

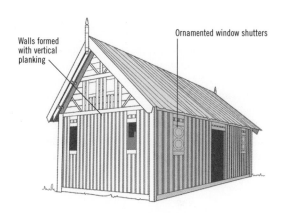

Walls formed with vertical planking

Ornamented window shutters

INTERNAL LAYOUT

The simple internal layout of the house is oriented around the four directions, which relate to the four major destinies. The bed is always placed in the northeast, while the unimportant objects and entrance are placed in the west. The positioning of the houses in the village follows similar principles.

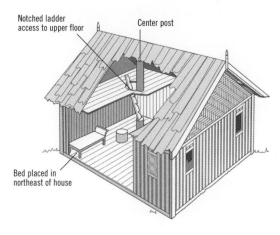

Notched ladder access to upper floor

Center post

Bed placed in northeast of house

DECORATIVE DETAILS

A woven wood door and carved wood panel are examples of the kind of handiwork for which the Zafimaniry are famous. Their finely chiseled geometric motifs on doors and windows reflect their beliefs. Two common motifs are a spiderweb pattern (which symbolizes family ties) and the honeycomb (symbolizing community life).

ZULU INDLU

The Zulu, who live mainly in the South African province of KwaZulu-Natal, are the country's largest ethnic group and their language is the most widely spoken. The traditional home of the Zulu is a thatched "beehive" dwelling known as an *indlu*. It is considered one of Africa's finest vernacular structures, both aesthetically beautiful and ingeniously constructed. The framework of the indlu, known as the *izingtungo,* consists of a ring of saplings that cross each other at right angles and are tied together at each intersection. The roof is supported by a series of upright posts, up to nine in a large hut, which carry curved lumber components that support the roof.

Mats of thatching grass are tied to the framework with braided grass loops and the whole thatch is then secured by a net of grass ropes running from the apex to the ground and in concentric rings parallel to the ground. The indlu is topped by a cylinder of grass matting, which forms a small finial poking out of the thatch. Access is gained by crawling through a small arched opening, approximately 3½ feet (1 m) high, made of stepped rings of thatch; the entrance is secured by a thick hide, a wicker screen, or a hinged wood door.

The interior of the hut is divided into the men's side, to the right of the door, and the women's to the left. The floor is made of a carefully smoothed and polished mixture of cow dung and termite-mound clay that is smeared on the ground, where it sets hard and is polished by a smooth stone. A third of the way between the entrance and rear, a circular depression serves as the hearth, surrounded by a raised molded rim. Smoke from the fire escapes out the door or through the thatch. A platform at the back of the hut is used to store the family's possessions, guarded by charms that the community's medicine man buried beneath it when the hut was built.

SEE ALSO

> Toda Hut,
  pages 100–1

> Balinese Kuren,
  pages 154–5

> Tzotzil Chukal Na,
  pages 140–1

MATERIALS

* Saplings, tied
  together, to form
  framework

* Wood posts and
  curved lumber
  components to
  support roof

* Grass for thatch,
  tied together with
  grass ropes

KwaZulu-Natal (KZN) consists of three main geographic areas: a narrow coastal plain; a central region of hilly plateaus; and two mountainous areas, one formed of basalt, the other of granite.

KWAZULU-NATAL,
SOUTH AFRICA

INDLU CONSTRUCTION

The construction of an indlu is a task that is jointly shared by the men and women of the Zulu. The men do the building, the women the weaving and thatching. Thatching methods vary between regions and tribes, and often include patterns created by the interweaving of grass ropes or withies (willow stems). The distinctive beehive shape and structure of the indlu was an early inspiration to the architect Buckminster Fuller, creator of the geodesic dome.

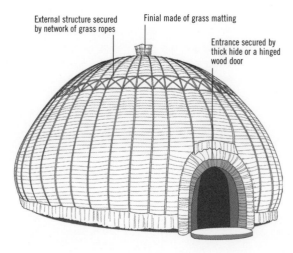

External structure secured by network of grass ropes

Finial made of grass matting

Entrance secured by thick hide or a hinged wood door

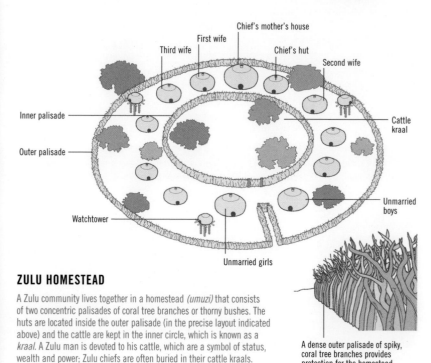

Chief's mother's house

First wife

Third wife

Chief's hut

Second wife

Inner palisade

Cattle kraal

Outer palisade

Watchtower

Unmarried boys

Unmarried girls

A dense outer palisade of spiky, coral tree branches provides protection for the homestead

ZULU HOMESTEAD

A Zulu community lives together in a homestead *(umuzi)* that consists of two concentric palisades of coral tree branches or thorny bushes. The huts are located inside the outer palisade (in the precise layout indicated above) and the cattle are kept in the inner circle, which is known as a *kraal*. A Zulu man is devoted to his cattle, which are a symbol of status, wealth and power; Zulu chiefs are often buried in their cattle kraals.

FROM ZULU INDLU TO THE "VENICE OF AFRICA"
NDEBELE PAINTED HOUSE

The extraordinary painted houses of the Ndzundza Ndebele have gained worldwide attention for their graphic splendor. Executed entirely by women, their powerful and colorful abstract designs have an interesting history. Archaeological evidence suggests that the various tribes of the Ndebele people originally lived in northeastern South Africa in simple thatched domes until the 1860s, when they moved to settle and intermarry with the Tswana and Pedi tribes. From the Tsawana they adopted a different form of dwelling—a cylindrical earth house that was topped by a conical thatch roof—which they began decorating initially in the style of the Pedi.

Fierce wars with the Boers in the 1880s resulted in all the extensive Ndebele lands being confiscated and the Ndzundza becoming indentured servants, a situation that lasted until the late twentieth century and parallels the situation of African slaves in the Americas. As a result, the Ndzundza people used the wall paintings on their houses to carry a message of cultural resistance, in the form of abstract colors and shapes—a secret language only understood by their fellow tribespeople. The white farmers considered this house decoration harmless and allowed the practice to continue.

The tradition of the Ndebele paintings has been maintained by the women of the tribe, because it is the responsibility of the wives to keep a well-decorated home. Over the decades, these paintings have evolved into an elaborate, symbolic communication system, based on a traditional palette of colors and forms, so that the paintings on each house speak of the history, beliefs, and identity of the family within. Pattern strategies were passed on from mother to daughter.

The modern world has affected the life and art of the Ndebele. They have appropriated and incorporated new symbols into their work and some of their women artists have become famous around the world. Their settlements near Pretoria have been absorbed by the city, and many Ndebele have adopted Western lifestyles.

SEE ALSO

> Cob House,
  pages 54–55

> Batammaliba
  Roundhouse,
  pages 110–11

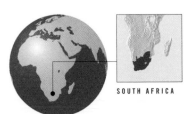

There are three main groups of Ndebele people: one group in Southern Transvaal, one group in Northern Transvaal, and one in Zimbabwe, known as the Matabele.

SOUTH AFRICA

MATERIALS

∗ Earth to build the
  main circular house

∗ Thatch to cover
  the conical roof

PAINTED HOUSES

The Ndebele painted earth houses take the form of a central drum, some 20–26 feet (6–8 m) in diameter, surmounted by a conical thatched roof. The central circular space was used by the parents as a sleeping area, with the left-hand side being the side of the woman, and the right side of the man. These two examples show the different styles of thatching used in different areas. Similarly, the designs on the outside walls vary from region to region. They are created and painted by Ndebele women using pigments derived from natural ochers, soot, and lime. The traditional painted houses now survive largely in scattered rural settlements.

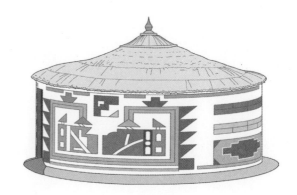

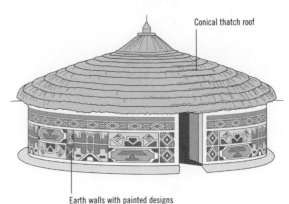

Conical thatch roof

Earth walls with painted designs

LATER RECTANGULAR DWELLINGS

In more modern times, Ndebele houses have evolved into rectangular dwellings, set in a courtyard, used by the women of the household for a variety of social functions. The courtyard is surrounded by walls that are elaborately painted with bold, geometric patterns.

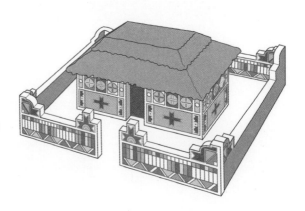

FROM THE PLAINS TIPI TO
FRONTIER LOG CABINS

The Inuit igloo and the Plains Indian tipi have immediate cultural resonance, and both are justly recognized as supreme examples of simple shelters of great ingenuity. Less well known are the striking forms of the Haida plank houses, decorated with vibrant paintings and crowned with the first totem poles. Log cabins come in all shapes and styles, as do the big barns of the North American landscape and the early settlers' building forms—the I-house, cracker house, and saltbox house. The Shakers devised their own architectural language of unadorned shape and form, which to this day remains highly influential. The adobe houses of New Mexico, designed for desert climates by the Pueblo peoples, have now become an internationally recognized style.

INUIT IGLOO

The igloo (a word derived from the Inuit term *iglu*) is a domed shelter built of snow blocks by the Inuit people of the far north. Igloos were originally built by only the Inuit people of Canada's Central Arctic regions and the Thule area of Greenland, but were later adopted by all Polar Inuit groups. The form of the igloo—a dome built without the use of any supporting structure—most likely evolved through trial and error over thousands of years.

Constructed in a variety of sizes, the best-known igloo is the smallest—the simple, snow-block dome, which could be constructed in a few hours to provide hunters with temporary shelter. Larger igloos provided semipermanent living accommodation during the winter months. In the summer, when the igloos started to melt, the Inuit lived in portable tents, framed with poles made of narwhal tusks and covered with sewn sealskins, which were more suitable for the warmer months. Extra-large snowhouses *(karigi),* up to 20 feet (6 m) in diameter, were built for ceremonies and feasts.

Once in use, heat from human bodies, from a stove, and lamps fueled by the oil from animal blubber rises and is trapped inside the snow dome, which has excellent insulating properties. The cold air sinks and is trapped in the entrance tunnel, built below the internal floor level. Thus the igloo remains comfortable and can maintain an internal heat level of 59.9° F (15.5° C) or more, when the outside temperature is far below freezing.

To prevent the snow shell from melting, igloos were sometimes lined with caribou skins, which would trap a layer of cold air above them and also serve as extra insulation. Over time, the igloo forms a smooth, airtight ice surface that also increases its structural strength, making it strong enough to support the weight of a person standing on its roof. An ingenious ancient invention, using the very simplest of available materials, the energy-efficient igloo is a prime example of vernacular building at its most effective.

SEE ALSO
> Mousgoum Tolek, pages 106–7

The Inuit Circumpolar Council (ICC), established in 1977, now represents the 150,000 Inuit people who live in the USA, Canada, Greenland, and Russia.

NORTHERN
CANADA/
GREENLAND

MATERIALS

* Snow blocks

* Sticks, bones, or broken paddles to insulate sleeping platform, over which is laid moss and sealskin (or preferably deerskin)

SPIRAL CONSTRUCTION

The igloo is built from the inside and constructed in a spiral. First, a central hole in the ground is excavated by cutting out even blocks of snow that has turned to ice, which are then arranged in a 16-foot (5-m)-wide circle around it. The first layer is then cut into a slight upward and inward curve.

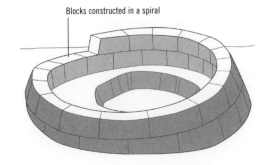

Blocks constructed in a spiral

BUILDING THE CURVE

The walls are built up using progressively smaller, overlapping blocks, shaved so that they gradually lean inward, and the dome is completed by a final key block, shaved until it fits exactly in the top hole. The dome is then covered with loose snow, which is rubbed into all the cracks between the blocks to seal them.

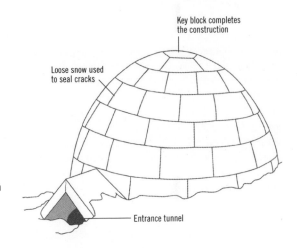

Key block completes the construction

Loose snow used to seal cracks

Entrance tunnel

CROSS SECTION

Once the dome is complete, a hole is cut under the wall to provide a cold sink, leading to a short roofed entrance tunnel. Inside the igloo, several blocks are used to create a living and sleeping platform *(iglig)*. The dome is pierced by small ventilation shafts to avoid the risk of asphyxiation.

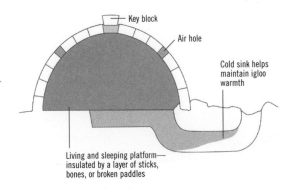

Key block

Air hole

Cold sink helps maintain igloo warmth

Living and sleeping platform—insulated by a layer of sticks, bones, or broken paddles

HAIDA PLANK HOUSE

The indigenous nation of the Haida has lived on the archipelago of the Queen Charlotte Islands, off the coast of British Columbia, and Prince of Wales Island, off the coast of Alaska, for between seven thousand and ten thousand years. These isolated peoples developed their own unique crafts and skills, introducing the first totem poles and building substantial war canoes—each made out of a single cedar tree and manned by some fifty warriors—used to carry out raiding missions. They were also superb carvers and artists. Contact with Europeans in 1774 had a dramatic impact on their way of life and their ability to survive according to their traditions. Hunter-gatherers and fishermen, they lived in small villages, consisting of one or more rows of plank houses, with the village chief's house at the center, strung along a beach between the ocean and the forest.

To the Haida, these plank houses, built of western red cedar, were central to their culture and contained the spiritual world of their ancestors. Much ceremony attended every aspect of house construction; it had to be aligned correctly and built in a certain order. There were two main types: the more common two-beam house, and the eight-beam house, found only on the Queen Charlotte Islands. The interior of the house was organized around a central open hearth in which a fire burned constantly. Small houses averaged 20 x 30 feet (6 x 9 m) and were occupied by thirty to forty closely related family members, while large houses were up to 50 x 60 feet (15 x 18 m), with twice as many residents, including extended family.

There are only two small surviving villages of Haida, at one of which, named Massett ("white slope"), the largest Haida house built since 1850 has been constructed. Known as Chief Weah's "Monster House," it is an eight-beam house, measuring 55 feet (17 m) square, which took two thousand people to build.

SEE ALSO

> Maori Meeting-House, pages 166–7

BRITISH COLUMBIA/ ALASKA COAST

The Queen Charlotte Islands form an archipelago of two main islands—Graham and Moresby—and 150 smaller ones. To the north is Prince of Wales Island, the fourth-largest island in the USA.

MATERIALS

* Western red cedar for structural framework of posts and beams

* Wood planking for walls

TWO-BEAM HOUSE

The basic framework of a Haida two-beam house, a large, gable-roofed structure, is built around four massive vertical posts, spanned by two huge round beams up to 50 feet (15 m) in length, the whole being covered with a cladding of wide planks.

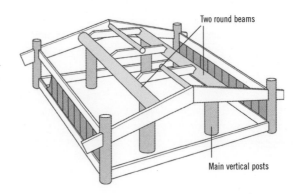

Two round beams

Main vertical posts

EIGHT-BEAM HOUSE

The eight-beam house is a more sophisticated structure, held together using mortise-and-tenon joints. The four substantial round corner posts are mortised to receive the tapered gable plates, which, in turn, support the heavy roof beams. These are cut with a flat underside to provide a stable, supported surface.

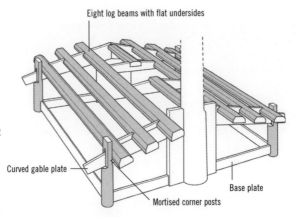

Eight log beams with flat undersides

Curved gable plate

Base plate

Mortised corner posts

HERALDIC POLE

The final act of constructing a Haida house is the erection of a heraldic pole at the center of the front of the building, bearing carvings of the mythological history of the clan who live in the house. The entrance is a hole made in the stomach of the crest animal that forms the pole's base. The outer posts also support carved figureheads, and the building's facade is highly decorated in the Haida style.

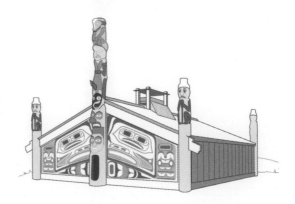

PLAINS INDIAN TIPI

The *tipi,* according to historian James H. Creighton, "is perhaps the most perfectly designed tent structure that has ever been used.... The conical home is as old as man and has multiple origins worldwide." Various forms of tipi-like shelters were certainly used by nomadic tribes across North America from earliest times, employing a basic structure of poles covered with whatever animal skins or natural material, such as barks and grasses, were on hand.

The tipi, or tepee—a structure familiar to most people from American westerns—used by the Indians of the Great Plains, such as the Sioux, was a relative latecomer, but is now considered the classic form. Its name derives from two Dakota Indian words—*ti,* "to dwell," and *pi,* "used for." (It should not be confused with a wigwam, also known as a *wickiup,* which is a domed single-room dwelling.)

The simple but elegant tipi is typically made up of just four elements—a set of sapling poles (lodgepole pine being ideal) that forms the basic structure, a semicircular cover made of skin or canvas, an inner lining, and a door flap. These are secured and bound together with rope and wood pegs, pins, and stakes.

The key innovations that enable tipi dwellers to have an open fire for cooking and heat inside the tent, without being smoked out, are the top opening and the smoke flaps (both of which are adjustable) and the inner lining, which is pegged up at a certain height around the bottom part of the tent. Air that comes in under the tent cover is funneled upward behind it, taking the smoke with it; the lining has the additional benefit of providing extra insulation.

The modern interest in tipis is generally acknowledged to stem from the seminal work *The Indian Tipi: Its History, Construction and Use* by Reginald and Gladys Laubin, first published in 1957. What was once the simple nomadic home of indigenous peoples has now been adopted across the world by tipi enthusiasts.

SEE ALSO

> Rendille Min, pages 112–13

> Sami Gamme and Goatte, pages 48–49

> Aboriginal Shelter, pages 164–65

The Great Plains of North America are defined as the vast area of prairies and steppes that lie east of the Rocky Mountains and west of the Mississippi River.

GREAT PLAINS, NORTH AMERICA

MATERIALS

* Wood poles to form the main structure

* Buffalo hide, later canvas skin, secured using wood lacing pins

TIPI STRUCTURE

The women of North American Indian tribes were responsible for making the tipis, choosing an appropriate site for them and erecting the structure. Erecting a tipi starts with tying together three main poles to form a triangular base. Ten or twelve additional poles, regularly spaced in a circle, are tightly tied to them. The canvas skin is then put in place, pulled down and around the framework and secured, using wood lacing pins to draw the seams together and pegs to hold it to the ground. A blanket serves to cover the entrance. The diagram indicates how the air flow is funneled up behind the lining to carry smoke from the fire up and out through the smoke flap.

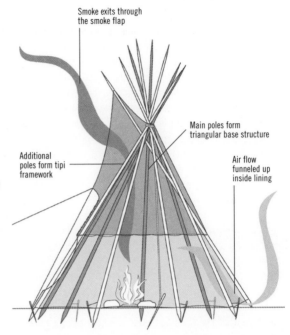

Smoke exits through the smoke flap

Main poles form triangular base structure

Additional poles form tipi framework

Air flow funneled up inside lining

TIPI INTERIOR

The egg-shaped interior of a typical tipi contains two beds with backrests; the cooking pots are kept in between them. The entrance is indicated by the dotted oval on left, with a firewood pile beside it. In the center is the fireplace, with the dotted shape indicating the smoke hole above it and the small square, the altar behind it.

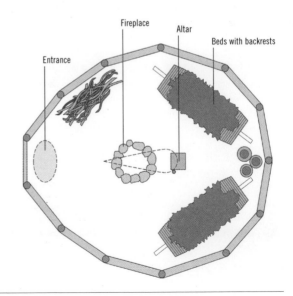

Fireplace

Altar

Beds with backrests

Entrance

BIG BARN

The barn is an essential feature of every farm in the United States and Canada—used to protect livestock and store grain—and its variety reflects the diverse building methods brought to this continent by the early European settlers. Nancy L. Mohr writes in the *The Barn: Classic Barns of North America* that "For centuries, farmers created barns from memory and experience, using the materials most readily available. They used whatever skills they had learned, considered the uses to which the barn would be put, remembered perfectly and imperfectly barns they had known, and threw themselves into solving problems."

Common to many farms was the giant of the form, the big barn, traditionally constructed with the help of friends and neighbors at a barn-raising ceremony, during which the preassembled framework of the barn was raised and put together in a single day. Such barns were completely utilitarian and rarely decorated; they were often painted "barn red," using a pigment of iron oxide, to protect the wood.

One of the most distinctive forms of barn in North America—and one of the rarest (less than one percent of the total)—is the round barn. George Washington had one in the 1700s, but the oldest surviving is the Hancock Barn, built by Shaker farmers in Hancock, Massachusetts, in 1824. Most were constructed between 1870 and 1920, of which about a thousand survive in the Midwest today.

In the early 1900s, an agricultural experiment station at the University of Illinois at Urbana-Champaign built three prototype round barns that triggered off a wave of construction in the state and across the Midwest. The experts claimed that such barns could be built using fewer materials, that they were more efficient to feed animals in, and were more stable in strong winds. In fact, they never became the dominant barn form; their efficiencies were overstated and the electrification of farms favored rectangular barns, which were much easier to wire.

SEE ALSO

> Hallenhaus House Barn, pages 56–57

USA/CANADA

The first ever census of historical barns, conducted by the U.S. Department of Agriculture in 2007, found there were 664,264 farm and ranch owners who had barns on their properties that had been built before 1960.

MATERIALS

* Wood for framework, wall, cladding, and roof shingles

BIG BARN

This big barn, with its metal grain silo, is built abutting a small hill, in the three-level German style that was common in the Michigan region. The style of roof (gambrel) provided more space for storing hay than traditional gable roofs. From this upper level, the hay was thrown down a chute to the threshing floor below.

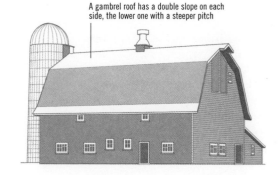

A gambrel roof has a double slope on each side, the lower one with a steeper pitch

CROSS SECTION

The middle floor of the barn served as both a granary and a threshing floor. It was linked to the silo and from here feed grain or corn could be thrown to the ground floor, where there were stalls for sheep and cattle and roosts for chickens.

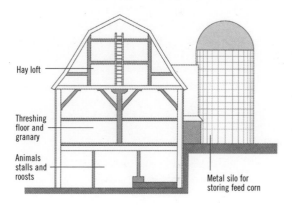

Hay loft

Threshing floor and granary

Animals stalls and roosts

Metal silo for storing feed corn

ROUND BARN

This is a section view of the twelve-sided Leonard barn near Pullman, Washington, in the Palouse region, one of the country's largest wheat-growing areas. Built entirely of wood in 1917, it has a giant shingle roof with dormers on both left and right. It is 60 feet (18 m) in diameter with a 10-foot (3-m)-high silo in the center.

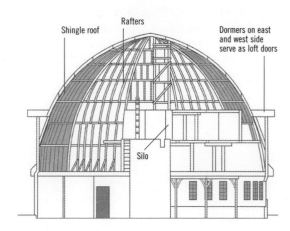

Shingle roof

Rafters

Dormers on east and west side serve as loft doors

Silo

I-HOUSE, CRACKER HOUSE, AND SALTBOX

These are three forms of "folk house," defined as a particular house type that has evolved through time, constantly being adapted and varying from place to place. The I-house came from seventeenth-century Britain, developed in the mid-Atlantic and southern states, and had spread across the United States by the mid-1800s. It was identified by Fred Kinffen, cultural geographer, in 1936, and was named the I-house because it was so common in the states of Indiana, Illinois, and Iowa—although he was eager to point out that it did not originate there and wasn't restricted to that area.

All I-houses are two rooms wide, one room deep, two stories high, and have side-facing gables with a symmetrical facade. Additional features varied from region to region and they were variously made out of logs, bricks, and stone. The basic form of the house would often be extended with a rear wing or a balcony.

A cracker house, in its simplest form, was a wooden shelter built by the early settlers in Florida and Georgia out of the abundant cedar and cypress they found there. These were kept off the ground by pilings made of rocks or bricks constructed from oyster shell and lime. To cope with heat and humidity, they were oriented for shade, had wide, covered porches, crawl spaces beneath for ventilation, and windows to catch cross breezes.

The saltbox house, which got its name from its sloping gable roof that resembled a wood box used to store salt in colonial times, is formed by a one-story addition across the rear of a one-and-a-half- to two-storey building. It was initially conceived as an easy method of enlarging a house, which may have been only a single room deep and housed a dozen or more people. Eventually, the saltbox house became an accepted building form, particularly in New England, where it was common before 1830, and it remained popular in other parts of the country until the late 1800s.

SEE ALSO

> Shaker-Style
  Buildings,
  pages 134–35

> Caribbean
  Chattel House,
  pages 142–43

MATERIALS

* I-house—variously made out of wood planking, bricks, and stone

* Cracker house—built entirely of wood. Pilings made of rocks or bricks, constructed from oyster shell and lime

* Saltbox house—variously made of wood planking, with brick chimney stack and stone foundations

Folk houses are scattered across the United States. I-houses are most commonly found in Indiana, Illinois, and Iowa; cracker houses originated in Florida and Georgia; and saltbox houses in New England.

USA

I-HOUSE

This English-style I-house is just one example of a form that contains numerous variations from region to region, and also reflects the different origins of its owners and builders. Among these variations are the materials from which it was built, the number and location of chimneys, and the layout of the rooms.

CRACKER HOUSE

The basic form of cracker house seen here—a simple square cabin with a broad veranda— was called a "single pen" house; when extended, it became known as a "saddlebag" or "dog-trot" house. The raised first floor was used to keep hunting hounds and chickens for food; the birds also provided a service by consuming fleas and other pests.

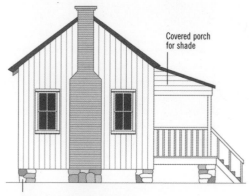

Covered porch for shade

Rock or brick pilings for foundations

SALTBOX HOUSE

The common features of the saltbox house are a central chimney and entrance and double-hung sash windows. In most saltboxes, the rear lean-to addition was divided into three rooms—a central kitchen with fireplace and oven, a room reserved for childbirth and nursing the ill, and a pantry.

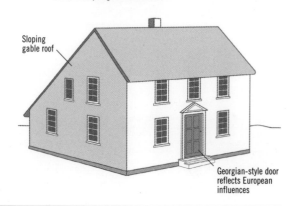

Sloping gable roof

Georgian-style door reflects European influences

LOG CABIN

The quintessential and rudimentary frontier dwelling, the log cabin, dates from 1638 in Colonial America, first being constructed by Finnish and Swedish settlers, on the site of what has now grown into Wilmington, Delaware. German and Ukrainian immigrants later arrived and brought their own log-building traditions. They were also built by the Scots and Irish, who had no tradition of building with logs but were skilled with stone masonry; log cabins were not widely adopted by the English. African-American slaves were housed in log cabins, as were some Native American tribal groups when forced into a sedentary way of life. The Hispanic settlers of New Mexico built them as farm buildings, often plastered with adobe.

The scale and other characteristics of the log cabin were largely determined by the length, variety, and abundance of the available lumber. The simplest and oldest forms of log cabin were constructed using round logs laid on top of each other and secured at the corner with basic notches. Inside the log cabin, in order to insulate it, the rounded logs that protruded from the wall had to be covered over and "chinked" to keep out drafts. The most common method was to fill the cracks with sphagnum moss and cover the whole with lime plaster. In some areas, scrap pieces of lumber were used to cover the gaps. As construction methods improved, the need for "chinking" was eliminated by a technique whereby the underside of a log was scooped out in order to fit tightly on the rounded log below.

A number of factors kept the tradition of building log cabins alive long after the days of the initial pioneer builders. Log construction was used for park lodges in the National Parks, and thousands more were built in forests and parks during the Great Depression. The log cabin has become a symbol of the nation's pioneering spirit, and is built into its history, folklore, myth, art, and song.

SEE ALSO

> Russian Izba,
  pages 62–3

> Zafimaniry House,
  pages 114–15

Log cabins, both traditional and modern, can be found in many, if not most, of the states.

USA

MATERIALS

* Logs for main structure

* Spaghnum moss and lime plaster to fill in gaps between the logs for insulation

* Wattle to make the chimney

* Stone or clay to make the hearth

SIMPLE LOG CABIN

Simple log cabins are generally just one story, 6–8 logs high, and have only a single room ("pen"), some 12–16 square feet (3.6–5 m sq) in area. There is one door, no windows, earthen floors, and a fireplace at one end of the cabin, with a wattle chimney and a stone or clay hearth. Roofs are generally supported by horizontal logs notched into the triangular-shaped gable wall end and then covered with hand-cut wood shingles.

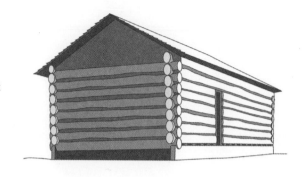

CORNER NOTCHES

Corner notches developed as a way of fitting the logs more securely and tightly together. The simplest and most widely used type is called saddle notching, but a huge variety of others were employed by different cultural groups.

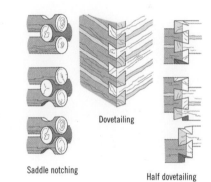

Dovetailing

Saddle notching

Half dovetailing

CONSTRUCTION

The simple and sturdy nature of the log cabin remains attractive and it is still a popular building form with a wide variety of modern uses. Whereas traditional log cabins would be built of round, hand-cut interlocking logs, they are generally now constructed from premachined lumber components, but still using interlocking corner joints.

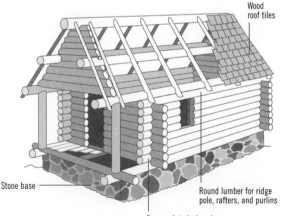

Wood roof tiles

Stone base

Round lumber for ridge pole, rafters, and purlins

Corners interlock, using traditional saddle notching

SHAKER-STYLE BUILDINGS

The vernacular style of the Shakers has been rightly celebrated and admired. Originally known as the United Society of Believers in Christ's Second Appearing, the movement was founded by Ann Lee in Manchester, England in 1747 and spread to North America in 1774, where, over the next century, the Shakers established and maintained nineteen communal settlements that attracted some twenty thousand converts. According to design writer Roger Shepherd, "There was no art of architecture among the Shakers; no written statement of style. But, there was certainly a definite sense of purpose in the particular religious doctrine and social organization of this unique community, which found expression in its building and design."

The basic standards that defined both the buildings and their interiors were simplicity and utility. The Shakers frowned on any kind of decoration, and they favored pure, clean forms that were highly functional and economical to make. The house interiors were bright and airy, well-heated and clean, uncluttered and serene.

As they believed Christ was both male and female, the sexes in Shaker communities were considered equal, but separate. They were also celibate, and maintained their communities through converts and adoptions. As the Shaker movement developed, they began to systematize the layouts of their communities. On the main street would be the Shaker meetinghouse, alongside other key community buildings, such as the infirmary and schoolhouse. Behind those buildings, running in parallel, were situated the houses, stops, and workshops of the sisters and brethren.

What enabled the Shaker style to grow and develop was the fact that all the unknown artisans involved were able to innovate, providing they held to the group's essential tenets. "This freedom to experiment in the interest of betterment," says Shepherd, "saved Shaker architecture from the blight of institutionalism or stereotype."

SEE ALSO

> I-House, Cracker House, and Saltbox, pages 130–31

The Shaker movement peaked at six thousand members in 1840, but went into almost total decline in the twentieth century. One Shaker community survives today in Sabbathday Lake, Maine.

EAST COAST, USA

MATERIALS

* Wood or brick walls
* Stone foundations

TYPICAL SHAKER HOUSE

This typical Shaker community dwelling was built to allow for minimum contact between men and women. It has two entrance doors, two staircases, and separate halls leading to the sleeping chambers, known as retiring rooms. Both sexes shared a common dining room, but ate at separate tables. Meetinghouses had three entrances, one for each sex and one for the ministry.

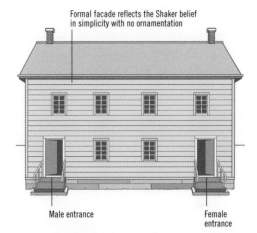

Formal facade reflects the Shaker belief in simplicity with no ornamentation

Male entrance

Female entrance

SHAKER STYLE

Shakers made their own furnishings, including chairs, cupboards, tables, beds, desks, bookcases, washstands, trunks, benches, stools, sewing boxes, brushes, and brooms. As in their architecture, they discarded any unnecessary ornament, creating furniture of simple forms and proportion. Rooms had white plaster walls lined with peg boards, on which their distinctive ladderback chairs could be hung when not in use.

BROTHERS' SHOP

This is the four-story brick Brothers' Shop at the Mount Lebanon Shaker Village in New Lebanon, New York—the largest and most industrious Shaker community in the United States from 1785 to 1947, and the movement's spiritual center in the country. At its peak, Mount Lebanon consisted of six hundred members with hundreds of buildings spread out over 9½ square miles (25 sq km).

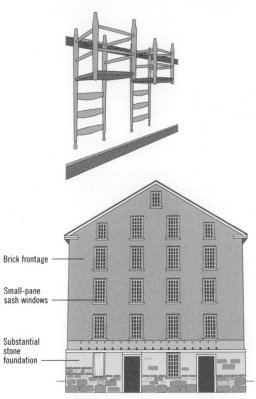

Brick frontage

Small-pane sash windows

Substantial stone foundation

NEW MEXICAN ADOBE HOUSE

The history of adobe building in New Mexico has its roots in a period (AD 700–1500) when the Anasazi peoples, who had previously been living in semiunderground pit houses, began building single-story houses on the ground, using layers of dried mud or of stones laid in adobe mortar, without windows and with flat roofs. From these simple structures, their culture and architectural skill developed. They built clustered settlements of stone and adobe—the most extensive of which, such as Chaco Canyon, accommodated some seven thousand people. For what were most probably ecological reasons, the Anasazi culture started to collapse around 1300 and many of the tribes moved to areas along the Rio Grande. Here, they began building smaller dwellings using sun-hardened sand and clay.

The early Spanish settlers called these adobe structures *"pueblo"* (after a Spanish word for village); the Zuni were renamed Pueblo Indians by them because of the prevalence of these structures within their communities. A simple adobe pueblo consisted of a log-frame building to which the adobe compound was applied as mortar. Later, the Pueblo Indians would be introduced by the Spanish to a method of shaping the adobe into bricks. Producing adobe bricks is simple. Mud (or a mud mixture) is carefully poured into a wood mold, which is lifted off when the newly formed brick is dry enough. When ready, the bricks are turned on their edge to complete drying. The word *adobe*, meaning "mud brick," dates back some four thousand years to Middle Egypt. In more modern English usage, the term has come to include a style of architecture popular in the desert climates of North America, especially in New Mexico.

In recent years, there has been an increased interest in building adobe homes in New Mexico and other Southern states because they are energy efficient and use natural materials. New Mexico Earth Adobes, which has one of the largest adobe yards in the world, claims to have made some fifteen million adobe bricks since 1972.

SEE ALSO

> Cob House,
  pages 54–55

> Great Mosque
  of Djenné,
  pages 104–5

> Yemen Tower House,
  pages 78–79

> Paisa House,
  pages 146–47

The first evidence of earth dwellings in the American Southwest dates from the fourth century AD.

NEW MEXICO, USA

MATERIALS

* Mud for cast adobe bricks and, mixed to a paste, for exterior "plaster" finish

* Wood posts and beams to make the basic framework

PRE-ADOBE HOUSE

This reconstruction of a semi-underground pit house of the Anasazi people is based on remains found in southern Colorado, dated AD 500–700. Although the Anasazi gradually moved into crude adobe shelters above ground, they retained and extended the form of the underground pit house to create spiritual spaces they called *kivas*.

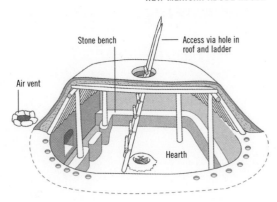

Air vent

Stone bench

Access via hole in roof and ladder

Hearth

SIMPLE ADOBE HOUSE

The posts extending out from the exterior walls are the ends of wood beams, inserted to support the immense weight of a flat earthen roof. Round spouts were also often placed at the base of the parapet surrounding the roof to drain off rainwater. This would run into a small trench left all around the internal edge of the roof, immediately inside its surrounding wall.

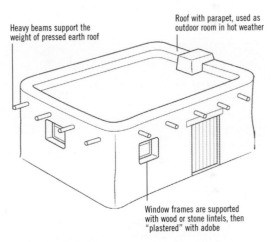

Heavy beams support the weight of pressed earth roof

Roof with parapet, used as outdoor room in hot weather

Window frames are supported with wood or stone lintels, then "plastered" with adobe

REVIVAL-STYLE SPANISH HOUSE

This is a comparatively elaborate design based around a number of internal spaces and verandas. Houses in this style were built from the mid-nineteenth century, and modern homes often copy their structure today. The building complex is enclosed by a wall with a central gate; within it is a series of one- or two-story units, all with flat roofs, and linked by covered verandas. Staircases are now internal, and the numerous windows are set very deep in the wall. The thick walls slope slightly inward from the base.

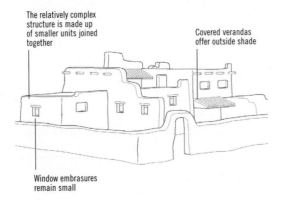

The relatively complex structure is made up of smaller units joined together

Covered verandas offer outside shade

Window embrasures remain small

FROM CHATTEL HOUSES TO
URUS REED HOUSES

In the mountains of southern Mexico, the Tzotzil people live in small villages of thatched dwellings with four-sided roofs, while in the Amazon the Yanomami combine their individual dwellings into one huge circular shabano. In the Caribbean, former African slaves invented the first mobile home, the chattel house, which could be disassembled and moved at short notice. In the highlands of Colombia, unique buildings combining bamboo structures with adobe and stone are being studied for their ability to survive earthquakes. High on Lake Titicaca in the Andes Mountains, the Urus people live on floating islands in houses made of reed. And in southern Chile, a unique set of wood churches has been recognized by UNESCO as a World Heritage Site.

TZOTZIL CHUKAL NA

The Tzotzil ("people of the bat") live at an altitude of 6,500 feet (2,000 m) in the west central region of the southernmost Mexican state of Chiapas, in a landscape characterized by pine-covered mountains and steep valleys. The largest indigenous group (292,000 people, according to the 2000 Mexican census) in the state, they are concentrated in ten *municipios* (main towns), surrounded by small hamlets, near the city of San Cristobal.

In the smaller communities, the most common house type is called a *chukal na,* which has wattle-and-daub walls and a steep, four-sided roof, thatched with grass. The house itself sits within a fenced compound, which may contain a shelter for animals, a granary, and a sweat house, alongside fruit trees, vines, flowers, and crops of corn or squash.

The interior of the house has no dividing walls, but living spaces are carefully defined according to the Tzotzil belief system. The main symbol of the Tzotzil culture is the sun, which is called "Our Father Heat," and their everyday activities are arranged according to a "thermal order of the cosmos," in which men are hot, women are cold, and the gods are the hottest of all.

Gary Gossen, who studied one Tzotzil community at Chamula, writes, "The importance of heat is ever present.... The daily round of domestic life centers on the hearth, which lies near the center of the dirt floor of nearly all houses. The working day usually begins and ends around the fire, men and boys sitting and eating to the right of the hearth, women and girls to the left."

Many of the Westernized Tzotzil now live in modern houses made of adobe brick or cement blocks roofed with tile. Most Tzotzil families make their living by subsistence farming and by raising domestic animals. Many Tzotzil women and girls weave and embroider textiles to sell to tourists in the cities. In recent years, many Tzotzil have joined the guerrilla Zapatista Army of National Liberation.

SEE ALSO

> Sami Gamme and Goatte, pages 48–49

> Toda Hut, pages 100–1

> Zulu Indlu, pages 116–17

> Abelam Spirit House, pages 162–63

MATERIALS

* Wood for load-bearing framework of posts and beams, topped by lattice of wood and bamboo lashed together with vines

* Wattle and daub for walls

* Grass for steep, thatched roof

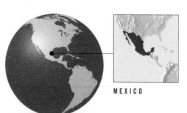

The state of Chiapas has a humid, tropical climate in lowland areas, and a temperate and foggy one in the mountains.

MEXICO

FRAMEWORK

To build this traditional single-room Tzotzil house, first a square load-bearing wood framework is created, consisting of oak or cypress posts, notched at the top to receive beams that are lashed to them with vines. A lighter lattice of thinner vertical posts and horizontal wattles, of wood or bamboo, is then added to it.

PYRAMID STRUCTURE

The ceiling is made of a square grid of light wood joists on which a pyramidal structure of six heavy wood rafters is built. It is held together by three square frames of joists at bottom, center, and top, which are then covered with a framework of wattle. Atop this is a small structure that serves as a ventilation hole to enable smoke to escape.

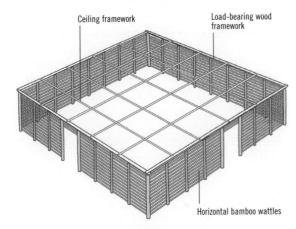

Ceiling framework

Load-bearing wood framework

Horizontal bamboo wattles

ROOF

The roof structure is then thatched with overlapping bunches of grass, which are tied to the wattles with vines.

Smoke hole for ventilation

Wattle structure to cover wood framework

Pyramid of rafters and joists

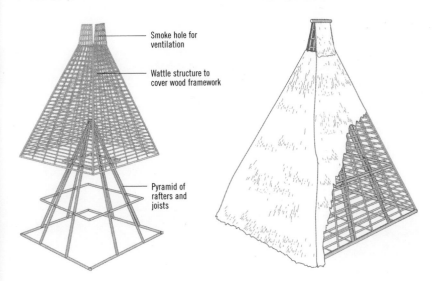

CARIBBEAN CHATTEL HOUSE

The chattel houses of Barbados and other parts of the British West Indies date back to the nineteenth century, and are possibly the world's first mobile homes. The word "chattel" means "movable property" and derives from "cattle"—at one time, this was the only significant piece of property a man would own. When the British finally freed the African slaves on the island in 1838, most continued to work in the sugar plantations, often journeying between different estates on the island. They lived on the margins of the plantation, on land they didn't own; therefore, the houses they built were small and designed to be easily dismantled and transported by cart to a new site, either at the end of a growing season, or in the case of a dispute with the plantation owner, who was their temporary landlord.

Chattel houses were built entirely of wood and assembled without nails to make them simple to disassemble and move from place to place. The wood was imported from the United States and was precut in length, which is why most of the chattel houses have similar dimensions, which range between 9 x 18 feet (2.8 x 5.5 m) and 15 x 30 feet (4.6 x 9.2 m). As the family expanded and perhaps became more settled, owners often added a couple of rear rooms, or even another house, onto the back.

Over the years, chattel houses acquired ornamentation, with open verandas, carved wood bannisters and trellis, decorative bargeboards, and elaborate fretwork around the windows. For many years, it was the tradition to paint chattel houses in beiges and browns, a fashion that has now changed to white or brighter colors.

In recent years, a new appreciation of the importance of chattel houses to Barbadian culture has enabled conservationists to save many historic chattel houses from dereliction for their heritage value. A large number still serve as family houses throughout the island.

SEE ALSO

> Russian Izba, pages 62–3

> Shaker-Style Buildings, pages 134–5

> I-House, Cracker House, and Saltbox, pages 130–1

The British West Indies refers to territories in and around the Caribbean that were colonized by the British.

BARBADOS AND THE WEST INDIES

MATERIALS

* Wood for basic structure, assembled with wood pegs

* Wood shingles and, later, corrugated iron for roof

TRADITIONAL CHATTEL HOUSE

The original chattel houses were simple two-room houses, twice as wide as deep, with a steep roof made of shingles (later corrugated iron), designed to survive the heavy rains and high winds of the hurricane season. They were set on limestone blocks rather than being anchored in the ground.

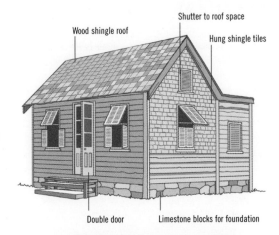

Wood shingle roof

Shutter to roof space

Hung shingle tiles

Double door

Limestone blocks for foundation

JALOUSIE SHUTTERS

For windows, the old chattel houses had shutterlike jalousies which had three sets of hinges—two vertical and one horizontal—that allowed maximum flexibility against the wind and sun. These were colloquially known as "jealousy shutters" because they kept the prying eyes of neighbors from seeing inside.

MODERN CHATTEL HOUSE

Many of the surviving chattel houses have been modernized with corrugated iron roofs, glass windows, and permanent foundations in order to provide comfortable and permanent homes.

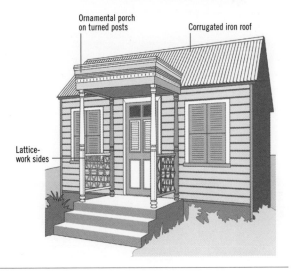

Ornamental porch on turned posts

Corrugated iron roof

Lattice-work sides

YANOMAMI SHABANO

The Yanomami (the word means "human being"), who live in the remote rain forests and mountains of northern Brazil and southern Venezuela, are one of the largest of South America's relatively isolated tribes. They had minimal contact with the outside world—through a limited number of missionaries, anthropologists, and government agents—until the mid-1980s, when gold miners illegally invaded their land, polluting the rivers with mercury and spreading malaria. In 2009, Survival International estimated the population of the Yanomami at approximately thirty-two thousand.

The semiagricultural Yanomami people hunt with bow and curare-tipped arrows and have a reputation for being aggressive, often staging raids on each other's settlements. They are organized around kin-base groups of varying size, related by marriage ties, who live together in a structure known as a *shabano*—a large, ring-shape structure enclosing a communal space.

The shabano is built in segments, each one constructed by the man and his family who are to occupy it. These individual family shelters *(nanos)* are then assembled in a ring and the gaps between them closed and thatched, except where an entrance is required. Finally, a defensive palisade is constructed in order to protect the entire shabano and its inhabitants.

Each Yanomami family nano has its own hearth, with hammocks, calabashes, and gourds hanging from the roof. Firewood is stacked at the back to form a wall. A small shabano may have six hearths and a diameter of 50 feet (15 m); an average shabano, accommodating eighty people, contains fifteen hearths and measures 100 feet (30 m) across. The largest, built to house 160 people or more, would be 200 feet (60 m) across. A shabano will last for a few years before it becomes infested with insects and starts to leak, then it will be burned to the ground and rebuilt.

SEE ALSO

> Black Tents,
  pages 76–77

> Abelam Spirit
  House, pages
  162–63

MATERIALS

* Hardwood poles to
  construct framework

* Saplings to create
  roof-canopy frame,
  bound together with
  vines or lianas

* Bisha palm leaves
  for roof thatch

The Yanomami live in the border areas between Brazil and Venezuela, one of the remotest parts of the Amazonian region.

**BRAZIL AND
VENEZUELA**

FRAMEWORK

The basic underlying structure of a large shabano is made up of a framework of hardwood poles, planted in two rows about 10 feet (3 m) apart. The outer row is of short posts approximately 5 feet (1.5 m) high; the inner row is twice that height. Individual family nanos are joined together to form the larger structure.

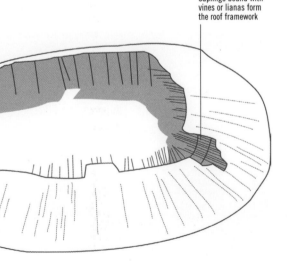

Roof-canopy frame of saplings

Individual family shelters (nanos) are built in segments

Two rows of hardwood poles form the framework

COMPLETED SHABANO

The shabano is completed with a roof-canopy frame made of slender saplings, which is cantilevered upward toward the center at an angle of thirty degrees. The saplings are bound together with vines or lianas, to which fronds of bisha palm are attached and overlapped to provide a weather-resistant thatch.

Saplings bound with vines or lianas form the roof framework

Thatch of bisha palm leaves

PAISA HOUSE

Paisa (short for *paisano*) is the name of the people and culture of the central mountainous region of Colombia, which was first colonized in 1785 by a mixture of people of Spanish descent, Native Indians, and free Africans. By 1904, they had established a network of eighty new villages, built in a striking and original manner that continues to be of great interest to architects and engineers in Colombia and elsewhere today.

The layout of these villages followed the European style, with a grid of streets and urban blocks, but, due to the difficult topographical conditions, they were built in a unique fashion in what is called the *bahareque* technique, in which the main construction material is local *guadua* bamboo, combined with wood and adobe.

There are no standard types in this architecture, but rather a set of elements that enable the building of a house to suit a wide variety of conditions; in some settlements, buildings reached a height of four or five floors. The use of additional elements, such as corridors and courtyards, tiled roofs, and decorative patterns varied according to the needs and status of the family concerned.

In recent years, guadua bamboo construction has been replaced by brick and concrete, but interest in the technique remains high. A major architect in Colombia, Dicken Castro, documented the paisa villages in the 1960s and 1970s, and others have built contemporary guadua buildings. One of the reasons for this continued interest is that these buildings survive earthquakes remarkably well. Workshops have now been established to spread the knowledge of how to grow and build with bamboo and keep these techniques alive.

An ardent advocate of bamboo construction is the Colombian architect Oscar Hidalgo-Lopez, who has not only built many bamboo buildings in various Latin American countries, but has also traveled the world to spread his knowledge, which is enshrined in a five hundred-page encyclopedia called *Bamboo: The Gift of the Gods*.

SEE ALSO
> Korowai Tree House, pages 160–61
> Toda Hut, pages 100–1
> Ganvié Stilt Village, pages 108–9

MATERIALS
* Bamboo for the basic structure of the house and as supporting scaffolding
* Wood for floors and platforms
* Adobe for walls, or concrete
* Tile and/or bamboo roof

Colombia is dominated by the Andes Mountains. Its main legal export throughout the twentieth century was coffee, which currently accounts for twelve percent of world trade by value.

COLOMBIA

MOUNTAIN PAISA

This paisa house, found in the mountainous coffee-growing zone of Colombia, known as Eje Cafetero, sits projecting out from a cliff, supported by an elaborate scaffolding, which, like the house itself, is made of bamboo. This long, rectangular building, divided into several rooms, housed the coffee workers. Surprisingly, it is earthquake-resistant because the bamboo has the capacity to absorb seismic energy and has a high bending strength.

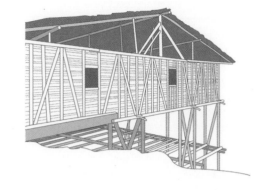

WINGED ROOF

The wood platform that forms the ceiling of the living quarters of the paisa house is used for the slow sun-drying of coffee beans. The roof of the house was either constructed from movable rails and could be slid back or, as pictured, had two wings that folded out for the same purpose.

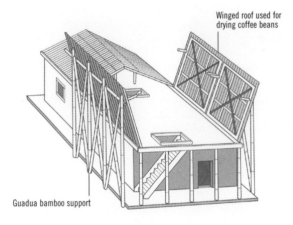

Winged roof used for drying coffee beans

Guadua bamboo support

MODERN PAISA CROSS SECTION

This cross section is of a modern two-floor Colombian bahareque house, made of guadua bamboo combined with adobe, wood, and concrete. The decorated "formal" front part of the house faces the street and is at ground level; the "informal" rear—the family's private space—is some 13 feet (4 m) above the ground, which slopes away beneath it.

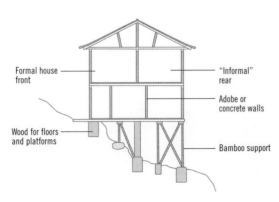

Formal house front

"Informal" rear

Adobe or concrete walls

Wood for floors and platforms

Bamboo support

URUS REED HOUSE

The ancient Urus people inhabited an extensive area around Lake Titicaca since before Inca times. They were later driven from their lands and forced to take refuge on man-made islands, in the high inland lakes of Bolivia and Peru. According to 2006 statistics, an estimated 320 families survive today on forty-four floating islands. The culture and life of the Urus traditionally revolves around the buoyant totora reed plant *(Scirpus totora),* from which they construct the islands they live on, their houses, and boats *(balsas)* with reed sails. The bulb and pith of the reed provide food for both the Urus and their animals, primarily pigs.

The island needs to be constantly replenished with fresh reeds because cut totora rots within six months, and even faster in the rainy season. The floating islands are built in two ways. One method involves tying a number of balsas together to provide a framework on which the cut reeds are piled up, the whole structure being anchored by ropes and stone to the bottom of the lake. The other technique is to tangle together an area of still-growing reeds and then pile cut reeds and soil on top; the latter is mixed with animal dung, both to add greater consistency and to act as a fertilizer.

The islands contain three main kinds of structure: the traditional rectangular reed houses, tipi-type structures that appear to be a modern development connected with increased tourism, and watchtowers of various kinds. The reed houses, built by women, are used mainly for sleeping to escape the freezing temperatures at night. During the day, the intense sun at some 13,000 feet (4,000 m) above sea level enables everyday life to be led in the open.

Traditionally, the Urus men fish from boats in the clear and deep icy waters of the 3,200-square-mile (8,290-sq-km) lake, and hunt in the bulrushes for waterbirds. The women spin, weave, cook, and tend small gardens in which potatoes are grown.

SEE ALSO

> Marsh Arab Reed House, pages 80–81

Located on the border of Peru and Bolivia, Lake Titicaca is one of the highest navigable lakes in the world (12,507 feet/ 3,812 m above sea level) and the largest lake in Latin America by volume.

BOLIVIA AND PERU

MATERIALS

* Floating islands of compacted reeds

* Totora reeds, either individual stems or bundles

* Reed mats, woven in layers, for walls

URUS REED HOUSE

Urus reed houses are rectangular in shape with a pitched gable roof and are constructed of individual reed stems or bound bundles, which may be attached to the island itself. The walls and roof are made of several layers of woven reed mats to keep out wind and rain.

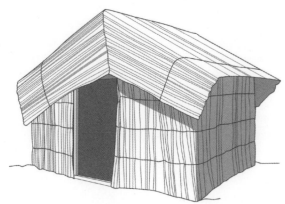

MODERN REED HOUSES AND WATCHTOWERS

These tipi-type structures and elaborate watchtowers are not traditional structural forms, but are, in part, a response to the growth in tourism, which has affected the lifestyles of the Urus people. New islands specifically designed for tourist visits have been created, and most islands now have their own motorboats, radios, and solar panels.

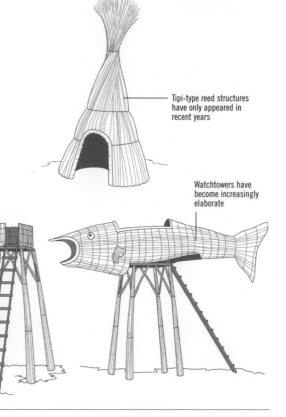

Tipi-type reed structures have only appeared in recent years

Watchtowers have become increasingly elaborate

A more traditional form of watchtower used as a defensive lookout

WOOD CHURCHES OF CHILOE

The remote, heavily forested Isla de Chiloé—the largest island of a scattered chain of the Chiloé Archipelago, off Chile's southern Pacific coast—is home to a remarkable set of wood churches, sixteen of which have been recognized by UNESCO World Heritage as "outstanding examples of the successful fusion of European and indigenous cultural traditions to produce a unique form of wood architecture." This unique vernacular typology is called the Chilota School of Religious Architecture in Wood.

This land of incessant rainfall and great natural beauty was originally inhabited by three native tribes—the Cuncos, Huilliches, and Chonos. The Spanish arrived on November 8, 1553, followed shortly thereafter by Franciscan and Jesuit missionaries, who were eager to evangelize. It was the Jesuit missionaries who first established the churches, the work being continued by the Franciscans after the Jesuits' expulsion in 1767. The Jesuits' plan to reach the scattered indigenous population was to send groups of missionaries on annual travels through the archipelago to convert the Indians and enlist them to build wood chapels at every stopping point on their journey.

An *amomaricaman* (attorney or deacon) was selected for a year to continue the spiritual and construction work while the priests were away. Thus the myths, spirits, and beliefs of the indigenous people became intertwined with the Catholic doctrine; this cultural fusion became enshrined in the unique wood structures that the Indians built under Jesuit instruction.

The churches were built using larch, coihue, and cypress, and assembled using wood pegs. The majority are located close to the coast, often with their backs to the mountains and facing south, as a protection from the rain. An estimated three hundred churches were built during the eighteenth century, ranging from small and simple country churches to larger and more elaborate structures. Of these, about eighty remain in various stages of repair.

SEE ALSO

> Wood Churches, pages 64–65

MATERIALS

* Wood for basic structure, using larch, coihue, and cypress; assembled with wood pegs

* Stone foundations to support wood columns

* Wood shingles *(tejuelas)* to cover roof; occasionally zinc

Chiloé Island is 118 miles (190 km) long and an average of 35–40 miles (55–65 km) wide. It is the second-largest island in Chile.

CHILOÉ ISLAND, CHILE

TYPICAL CHILOÉ CHURCH

Most of the churches of Chiloé follow a characteristic pattern. The rectangular basilica is divided into three naves by wood columns on stone foundations, and roofed with wood shingles called tejuelas. There is a tall, symmetrical tower, containing a belfry topped by a cross, a roofed entrance portico, and a pediment.

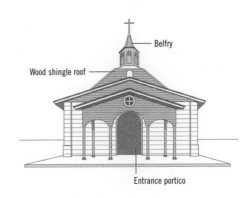

Belfry

Wood shingle roof

Entrance portico

OLDEST CHURCH

The Iglesia Nuestra Señora de Loreto de Achao is considered the jewel of Chiloé's wood churches. The oldest Jesuit church on the island, it was built between 1730 and 1767 using native woods. It was named a national monument in 1951.

THREE-TOWER CHURCH

This unusual three-towered church, the Iglesia de Tenaún, was constructed by Franciscan friars in 1837. Its main three-tier tower is balanced by two smaller ones at each end of the porch, which has squared columns. It was later remodeled in a neoclassical style, and its shingle roof replaced with zinc.

FROM BALINESE KUREN TO
MAORI MEETINGHOUSES

The scattered islands of Oceania have each developed their own style of vernacular buildings. They range from the octagonal houses of the Kalinga and the umbrella-shape fale tele of Samoa to the boat-shape dwellings of the Toraja and the extraordinary spirit house of the Abelam. In Bali, courtyard houses encompass an entire extended family's dwellings. In New Guinea, the Korowai people are still living in tree houses. In Australasia, Maori meetinghouses are alive and vibrant in modern times, whereas the many and various Australian Aborigine shelters have virtually disappeared.

BALINESE KUREN

The traditional Bali house *(kuren)* consists of a number of individual buildings on a square plot of land, completely contained in a high-wall compound, where a large family group or a number of related families lives together. Such vernacular homes share a number of similar features designed to accommodate the climatic conditions, particularly important during the hot and wet monsoon season.

They are largely built of lumber, of post-and-beam construction, are open to the elements, and employ a variety of elaborate roof shapes in the Javanese style. Villagers help each other to erect these self-built structures with the occasional help of a master carpenter.

The buildings sit on stone or square brick footings, with a masonry platform and stone bases for hardwood pilings, which are less affected by dry rot and termites. The floors are raised off the ground to enable breezes to cool the house from below, to keep food and belongings away from dampness, and to protect the occupants from malarial mosquitoes.

In the upper part of the house, lighter woods or bamboo are used for the nonload-bearing walls, fitted together using mortise-and-tenon joints secured with wood pegs or tied. Several windows provide cross ventilation. The large roofs, supported on piles, have a steep pitch with broad overhanging eaves, protecting the house from tropical rainstorms and direct sunlight. They are usually topped with thatch of rice straw, dried grass, sugar palm, or coconut leaves.

Traditionally, the Balinese people strive for a natural balance and harmony in their lives and their architecture; their buildings have a balance between male and female, negative and positive, sacred and profane elements. All Balinese house compounds follow the same fundamental plan. Traditionally, the only difference between the houses of different castes lies in the level of workmanship, the materials used, and the size and richness of the family temple.

SEE ALSO

> Zulu Indlu,
  pages 116–17

> Japanese Minka,
  pages 86–87

> Kalinga
  Octagonal House,
  pages 156–57

MATERIALS

* Stone or brick
  for foundations

* Hardwood for
  pilings

* Wood framework,
  post-and-beam
  construction

* Bamboo for the
  lighter upper walls

* Rice straw, dried
  grass, sugar palm,
  or coconut leaves
  for thatch

Bali is the biggest tourist destination in Indonesia and is home to most of Indonesia's Hindu minority.

BALI, INDONESIA

HOUSE AND COMPOUND

Balinese house compounds bind together village and community life, providing a focal point for family groups and for shared religious and cultural practices.

Guest pavilion
(Sakenam)
The guest pavilion for relatives and children varies in size, depending on how many need to be housed

Ceremonial pavilion
(Bale dangin)
The east pavilion is the place where the life rites and death rituals are held

Granary
(Lumbung or Jineng)
The storage area for rice

House temple
(Sanggah or merajan)
The place to worship the ancestors and their Hindu gods

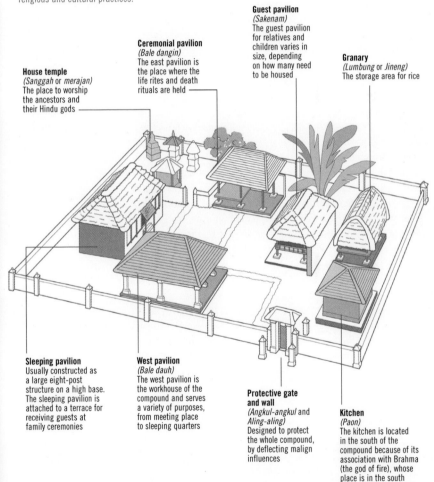

Sleeping pavilion
Usually constructed as a large eight-post structure on a high base. The sleeping pavilion is attached to a terrace for receiving guests at family ceremonies

West pavilion
(Bale dauh)
The west pavilion is the workhouse of the compound and serves a variety of purposes, from meeting place to sleeping quarters

Protective gate and wall
(Angkul-angkul and Aling-aling)
Designed to protect the whole compound, by deflecting malign influences

Kitchen
(Paon)
The kitchen is located in the south of the compound because of its association with Brahma (the god of fire), whose place is in the south

KALINGA OCTAGONAL HOUSE

Unique to the landlocked rice-growing province of Kalinga in the Philippines is the octagonal house, one of the earliest accounts of which was written by the German scientist Alex Schadenberg in 1887, who recorded that these houses were painted on the outside with "round designs or figures, representing men and women with strongly marked genital parts." Known locally as a *binayon* or *finaryon,* the octagonal house was "well known to every traveler down the Chico River," reported historian William Henry Scott in 1960. A generation ago, wrote Scott, the octagonal house "was considered the dwelling of the rich, and square houses less aristocratic, although this attitude has disappeared as the wealthy have more come to build non-Kalinga-type modern houses."

The octagonal house is traditionally about 20 feet (6 m) long and 17 feet (5.2 m) wide. The internal structure is defined by four short posts, sunk into the ground, that support the main rectangular living area about 4 feet (1.2 m) above the ground. The outer octagonal shape is defined, in turn, by eight outer posts, which stand on stones and are tall enough to support the roof. The height from the ground to the roof ridge is about 15 feet (4.5 m). Girders and joists pass over these posts to support the floor laths, while grooved beams on the eight outer posts receive the wall boards.

The living area, accessed by a ladder, is divided into three parallel sections running front to back, the middle portion being lower than the sides. The floor, which is covered with a bamboo mat that can be easily rolled up and taken to the river for washing, is not a perfect octagon because not all of the corners are floored.

The interior appears surprisingly spacious because of the exposed structural frame of the walls and roof, although in some houses the roof space is used as a loft or granary. The arrangement and size of these houses are well suited to the needs of an extended family.

SEE ALSO

> Samoan Fale Tele,
pages 168–69

> Toda Hut,
pages 100–1

> Balinese Kuren,
pages 154–55

MATERIALS

* Lumber for the internal wood framework; wood planks for the walls from floor level to eaves

* Plaited bamboo for walls from ground to floor level

* Thatch

Kalinga province is situated in the Cordillera Administrative Region in Luzon, the northernmost part of the Philippines.

THE PHILIPPINES

OCTAGONAL HOUSE

The distinctive Kalinga house has walls of braided bamboo mats from ground to floor level. The walls from floor level to eaves are of wood boards placed horizontally or vertically. The building is crowned by a thatched, hipped roof with eaves that form a rough-edged circle. The ground floor of the house is used as an open working space.

FLOOR PLAN

This plan of a typical octagonal house clearly shows the interior layout of the first-floor living area. The main lower platform has a raised bed area to the right, and a cooking and food storage area on the left next to the fireplace, which is slightly raised. The open space on the lower left runs from ground to roof.

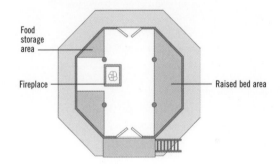

Food storage area

Fireplace

Raised bed area

CROSS SECTION

This cross section shows the internal wood framework of a typical finaryon-style house built in the early twentieth century. Three floor joists, two girders, and four posts form the foundation of the house. Notice that the braided bamboo walls are supported by logs, which were designed to prevent intruders or attackers from digging under the walls.

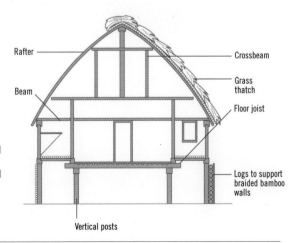

Rafter

Crossbeam

Grass thatch

Beam

Floor joist

Logs to support braided bamboo walls

Vertical posts

TORAJA TONGKONAN

In the remote, mist-shrouded mountain valleys of central Sulawesi, on an island in the Indonesian archipelago formerly known as Celebes, live the Sa'dan Toraja people, who build the extraordinary ancestral houses they call *tongkonan,* the form of which, some claim, dates back to Neolithic times.

The basic house is made of wood planking, assembled in tongue-and-groove formation without nails, which sits on solid, tree-trunk pilings, high enough to safeguard against rodents and snakes. This construction is topped by an outsize and outlandish saddleback roof, covered in thatch or, in modern times, with corrugated iron or zinc. The roof is constructed of an under-roof section of bamboo poles, tied to the rafters, over which are put overlapping layers of bamboo staves, tied together with rattan. In some cases, the roof extends so far that a giant post is necessary to support its extremity.

There is a great deal of speculation as to how this style developed. One view is that tongkonan symbolize and are shaped like the boats in which the Toraja people emigrated from Cambodia; others claim that it was boat-building technology, rather than symbolism, that drove the design of the sail-like roof. Others claim the roof shape is based on that of a buffalo's horn, an animal that the Toraja worship and consider a symbol of fertility and strength. They decorate the gables of their houses with these horns as a mark of status.

In contrast to the dramatic facade, the interior of the house is quite simple, usually consisting of three rooms—a living area, kitchen, and sleeping quarters. The cooking is done in a large fire pit, the smoke from which blackens the inside due to the absence of a chimney. Both exterior and interior are highly decorated with patterns and symbols related to the worship of ancestors in both carvings and paintings. In a village, these houses are arranged in a row facing north, in hierarchical order, each opposite a rice barn, which is built in a similar manner.

SEE ALSO

> Log Cabin,
  pages 132–33

> Korowai Tree House,
  pages 160–61

MATERIALS

★ Wood planking for main structure and tree-trunk pilings

★ Bamboo poles and staves, tied with rattan, for the under-roof area

★ Thatch, stone tiles, wood shingles or corrugated iron or zinc for saddleback roof

SULAWESI,
INDONESIA

Sulawesi, one of the Sunda Islands of Indonesia, is the eleventh-largest island in the world. Its population of fourteen million people has been troubled in recent years by bombings and violent riots between Muslims and Christians.

HOUSE OF ORIGIN

The "house of origin" is the cultural focus for the Toraja; its name, tongkonan, derives from the Toja word meaning "to sit," which reflects its purpose. It is a place where family members meet to take part in ceremonies or discuss important affairs. It consists of three basic elements: the wood piles, on which sits a log-cabin-type structure, topped by a thatched saddleback roof.

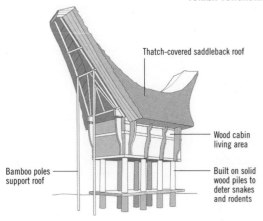

Thatch-covered saddleback roof

Wood cabin living area

Bamboo poles support roof

Built on solid wood piles to deter snakes and rodents

CONSTRUCTION

Constructing a tongkonan is a time-consuming and complex business, requiring skilled craftsmen. The pilings and the framework of the cabin are fabricated separately and taken to the building site for final assembly. Here, the roof is under construction, its dramatic gables supported by bamboo scaffolding.

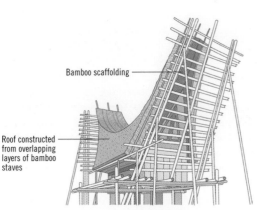

Bamboo scaffolding

Roof constructed from overlapping layers of bamboo staves

ROOF SUPPORT

This underside view of the flaring roof shows the giant post support decorated with buffalo horns, symbolizing the Toraja's sacred animal. The highly decorated facade is incised with geometric designs and classic motifs of cockerels and buffalo heads. In accordance with the Toraja's strict hierarchical society, the decoration used must be appropriate to the owner's social station.

KOROWAI TREE HOUSE

The Korowai—one of the few tree-house-dwelling peoples left in the world—live in the remote rain forests of Irian Jaya (now West Papua, an independent province of Indonesia since 2003). They were first seen by the outside world on October 4, 1978, and initial contact was made only in the 1980s. Their current population is estimated at 2,500. The Korowai are a people defined by their collective language *(koluf-aup)* and are organized in tight-knit clans; they live in small family groups and survive as hunter-gatherers.

Their staple foods are bananas and sago—the starchy pith of the sago palm—which is made into pancakes; the main ritual of their community life is the sago grub feast. This is supplemented by the domestic pigs that the women raise and the wild pigs and cassowaries that the men hunt. Both men and women fish. They also eat snakes, insects, forest fruits, and leaves.

Their tree houses are a practical response to their environment, because they live in an area of about 232 square miles (600 sq km) of low-lying swampy land between two major rivers that are prone to flooding. They are also built for security. There are some 250 indigenous tribes in the region, and intertribal warfare is rife; head-hunting raids by rival tribes have been common. The Korowai also believe the tree houses protect them from demons.

The Korowai build most of their tree houses 26–40 feet (8–12 m) above the ground; some tree houses as high as 148 feet (45 m) have been recorded. These elegant structures, usually built two or three together in a clearing, are strong enough to house a family of ten with their possessions and animals. They can also last for about five years with very little maintenance.

Recent years have seen dramatic changes for the Korowai, because many of them have been forced by the Indonesian government to move to mixed-clan communities and live in kampong stilt houses no more than 7 feet (2 m) above the ground.

SEE ALSO

> Toraja Tongkonan,
  pages 158–59

> Paisa House,
  pages 146–47

> Ganvié Stilt Village,
  pages 108–9

MATERIALS

* Wood spars for the floor base, covered with bark

* Sago palm provides shafts for wall frames and rafters and leaves for the thatch

Papua, the largest province of Indonesia, comprises most of the western half of the island of New Guinea and nearby islands.

WEST PAPUA, INDONESIA

CONSTRUCTION

Once a suitably large wamboon or banyan tree has been selected, construction begins with the floor base, which is made of tightly packed wood spars covered with the bark of the nibong or dal tree, supported by four to ten poles held firmly in the ground and tied together with rattan. The sago palm provides shafts for the wall frames and roof rafters, and leaves for the thatch on the long, winged roof. Access is gained by climbing up a notched pole. The entire structure is built using only stone axes and bone knives.

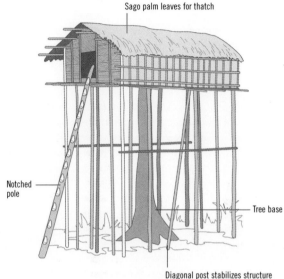

Sago palm leaves for thatch

Notched pole

Tree base

Diagonal post stabilizes structure

HIGH-LEVEL TREE HOUSE

The height at which the Korowai build their houses is related to the level of threat they feel from rival clans; when tension is lower, they feel safe enough to build closer to the ground. The effort involved in building a high-level tree house must be considerable; the access, via a set of vertiginous rudimentary ladders, is also designed, the Korowai claim, to prevent "sorcerers" from climbing the stairs.

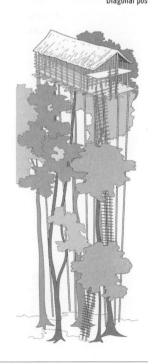

FROM BALINESE KUREN TO MAORI MEETINGHOUSES
ABELAM SPIRIT HOUSE

Dramatic "spirit houses" can be found throughout the Sepik River area, which stretches far inland from the northern coast of east Papua New Guinea. Of the many different tribal groups in the area, the most enthusiastic spirit house builders are the forty-two thousand Abelam people, who live in mountainous land, mainly covered by tropical forests, in the Maprik district of East Sepik province. The Abelam villages are dominated by these dramatic A-frame buildings, with their apexed roofs and elaborately painted facades. Measuring up to 100 feet (30.5 m) in length, with 60-foot (18.2-m)-high facades, these ceremonial houses are the central site of tribal life.

The Abelam call these houses *korambos,* consider them to be the dwelling place of their ancestors, spirits, and gods, and use them for male initiation ceremonies. They are aligned in relation to the daily course of the sun. Ethnographer Anthony Forge, who lived among the Abelam for two years in the early 1960s, counted more than one hundred spirit houses within a 5-mile (8-km) radius of his base village. He also recorded that the Abelam's neighbors built fifteen in just one six-month ceremonial period.

Korambos are elaborately adorned on the inside with wood carvings and sculptures, and on the facade with intricate patterns painted in bright colors. The various images that adorn the building have complex associations with the sacredness of the human body (eyes, navels, breasts), with animals, such as flying foxes and fireflies (believed to be the spirits of ancestors), and with the cult of the yam, which symbolizes nourishment and fertility. Regular yams are the staple food of the Abelam, but long ceremonial yams are grown in secluded gardens by the so-called Big Men of the village and are used in rituals and exchanges with rival Big Men.

SEE ALSO

> Rendille Min,
  pages 112–13

> Tzotzil Chukal Na,
  pages 140–41

> Yanomami Shabano,
  pages 144–45

MATERIALS

* Bamboo poles for
  main structure,
  tied with rattan

* Sago palm ribs
  for the entrance

* Sago palm fronds
  for thatch

**PAPUA NEW
GUINEA,
INDONESIA**

East Sepik, a province of Papua New Guinea, covers an area of about 16,525 square miles (42,800 sq km). The Sepik River is one of the largest rivers in the world in terms of water flow.

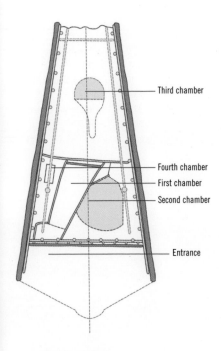

Third chamber

Fourth chamber
First chamber
Second chamber

Entrance

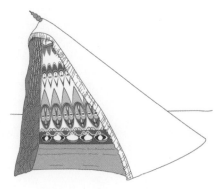

KORAMBO OR SPIRIT HOUSE

The elaborate facades of the spirit houses are painted in intricate patterns and in vivid colors under the direction of a master artist. Large and small male faces and figures represent clan ancestors. These are connected by energetically executed zigzag patterns. The bamboo framework of the korambo can be seen below.

CROSS SECTION

To gain the power and magic needed to grow long yams, male initiates undergo rituals, which culminate in a "journey" through the spirit house. They crawl through a low entrance into the first narrow chamber, which leads on to the second, containing a large wood figure. The large third chamber has a 6½-foot (2-m)-high figure sitting in the center of a dark space. In the fourth chamber, men use sacred musical instruments to provide the "voice" of the spirit house.

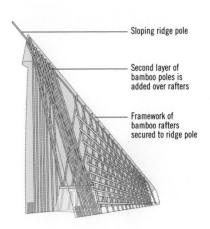

Sloping ridge pole

Second layer of bamboo poles is added over rafters

Framework of bamboo rafters secured to ridge pole

ABORIGINAL SHELTER

In 1997, the most detailed study ever undertaken on Aboriginal architecture—*Gunyah, Goondie & Wurley,* by Australian anthropologist Paul Memmott—was published. His findings have overturned the notion that Aborigines lived only in makeshift huts or lean-tos—an argument used by European settlers to claim that Australia was *terra nullius,* or empty land. It also debunked the stereotype of Aborigines as mere "primitives"; in fact, they should be considered the world's first architects, because they displayed considerable ingenuity in providing shelter and accommodation in a minimal manner—virtually no examples of which survive today.

There are five hundred different Aboriginal peoples in Australia, each of which has its own language and territory and had its own style of shelter. The technologies that were utilized in the construction of these shelters would have included, says Memmott, "thatching, grass plaiting, clay and mud plastering, excavated floors, earth platforms, sand-weighted roofs, split cane ties, and the weaving of foliage between wall rails." They served many different purposes and varied with the seasons. Some were simple overnight shelters, while others saw more permanent use. Their size, shape, and nature varied depending on tribal traditions, the weather, and how many people needed to be accommodated.

In the desert regions, when the weather was clement, simple windbreaks were most common, providing protection from the sun during the day and from the breezes at night. When the rains came, domed huts with grass roofs were built. During the wet season in various parts of northern Australia, roofed platform houses were constructed. If the mosquitoes got too bad, igloolike domes, made of a sapling frame and covered with paperbark, were built in order to escape the insects' unwelcome attention.

SEE ALSO

> Rendille Min,
pages 112–13

> Ganvié Stilt Village,
pages 108–9

> Sami Gamme
and Goatte,
pages 48–49

> Mongolian Ger,
pages 94–95

> Plains Indian Tipi,
pages 126–27

MATERIALS

* Round wood for internal frame and support, along with split cane ties

* Clay and mud plaster for walls

* Grasses and woven foliage for roofing

Tribal Aborigines still live a traditional life in remote areas of northern, central, and western Australia.

AUSTRALIA

DOMED HUT

This kind of domed hut, built on a framework of lawyer cane covered with blady grass, was common in the rain forests of tropical Queensland and northern New South Wales. High enough to stand up in, it was used by families for extended periods during the wet season.

PLATFORM SHELTER

Platform shelters, built as a living and sleeping area during the rainy season, featured a basic structure of sapling poles, supporting a wood platform some 6 feet (1.8 m) above the ground, roofed with curved sheets of eucalyptus bark. The sloping pole was the only access. A smoky fire underneath the shelter helped keep mosquitoes at bay.

"HUMPY" SHELTER

This more tentlike form of shelter, known as a "humpy," is made of a framework of sticks covered with sheets of soft paperbark that could easily be stripped from the trees. The softness and flexibility of the paperbark made it extremely useful also for sleeping mats, to line cradles, and as bandages. Aborigines also used the leaves of the tree for medicinal purposes, chewing them in order to relieve headaches.

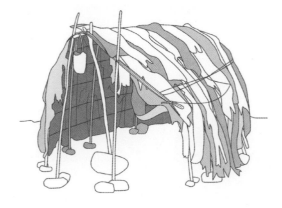

MAORI MEETINGHOUSE

Meetinghouses, which can be seen throughout New Zealand's North Island, evolved from the pre-European sleeping houses of the Maori chiefs and came into their own from 1870 onward as a way of reasserting Maori culture in reaction to colonization. In addition, according to the anthropologist Alfred Gell, this was a period when, unable to compete through traditional warlike means, Maoris focused their competitive spirit "on the construction of large, elaborately carved and painted meetinghouses, each Maori community trying . . . to outdo its neighbors and rivals." Other authorities suggest that these buildings replaced the war canoe as a focus of group pride.

The two main types of meetinghouse—which are known as *whare nui* (big house) and *whare whakairo* (carved and decorated house)—both follow the same common ground plan. The size and amount of ornamentation on the house say something about the *mana* (prestige) of the extended family or tribe that built it. The meetinghouse sits within a compound *(marea),* alongside other buildings, facing an open space that is used for Maori ceremonies.

Each meetinghouse is not only named after an ancestor, but the building itself represents the body of the ancestor as well. The figure or mask *(koruru)* at the junction of the eaves of the veranda represents his face, the porch his brain *(roro),* the front window his eye *(mataaho).* The bargeboards *(maihi)* that make up the eaves are his arms, held out in welcome, and usually tipped with fingers *(raparapa).* The interior of the meetinghouse is his chest (*poho*), the ridge pole *(taahuhu)* his spine, and the rafters *(heke)* his ribs.

Further ancestors are depicted in the wall carvings; in modern meetinghouses, photographs of recent ancestors adorn the walls in their stead. Meetinghouses have been constantly adapted to suit the needs of succeeding generations and new ones continue to be built, providing a focus for modern-day Maori culture.

SEE ALSO

> Haida Plank House, pages 124–25

MATERIALS

* Lumber for the wood framework

* Wood clabboard siding for the outside walls and the deep porch with its carved framework

* Carved wood panels and panels woven from flax and reeds for internal walls

* Thatch and corrugated iron for roofs

According to the latest theories, it is now believed Maoris arrived in New Zealand a thousand years ago.

NEW ZEALAND

MEETINGHOUSE

The meetinghouse is a structure that has evolved from earlier chiefs' houses into a communal building for a *whanau* (extended family group) or *hapu* (subtribe) to gather in. It is a large rectangular building, ranging in length at 40–98 feet (12–30 m), typically with a gabled corrugated iron roof, walls of wood clapboard siding, and a deep porch fronted by an elaborately carved framework.

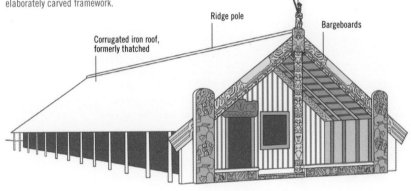

A *tekoteko*, a carved human figure, representing the ancestor of the house, whose threatening character deters enemies

Ridge pole

Bargeboards

Corrugated iron roof, formerly thatched

INTERIOR

In the one large space inside, there are two significant carved posts that support the ridge pole, which represent *Tane* (Life Giver) and *Hinenuitepo* (Death). The walls have alternating wood carved panels and patterned panels woven by the women from flax and reeds in geometric designs. The rafters are painted with elaborate patterns in black, red, and white.

FROM BALINESE KUREN TO MAORI MEETINGHOUSES
SAMOAN FALE TELE

The *fale tele* or "round house" is found only on the islands of Samoa and was traditionally used as a meetinghouse. The fale is one of the most elegant and airy of all vernacular structures. John Charlot, in *Esthetics of the Samoan Fale,* writes: "The *fale* has the still, perfect beauty of a round Japanese lantern, a globe lamp, or a soap bubble. But it has also a monumentality that, combined with its lightness, makes it unique in the history of art."

The unusual construction aspect of the fale tele is that it is totally supported by the wood columns in the center, in a similar way to an umbrella, rather than by the posts that ring the outside. It is also produced without using a single nail, relying instead on bindings of coconut fiber *(afa),* of which an estimated 39,370 feet (12,000 m) are required for an ordinary native house.

The fale's sides are open to the elements, but blinds made from woven palm leaves are used to close them off when necessary. The floors of the fale are covered with crushed coral, overlain with woven palm mats. The building of a fale tele was a matter of great ceremony, and was carried out only by a member of the Samoan guild of builders *(tufunga),* who used no plans, but solely relied on his judgment and experience. Other forms of fale include *Fale O'o,* "Small House," and *fale folau,* or "Long House," used as a residential guesthouse and for meetings of the family. Small beach fales for tourists are now a common sight on the Samoan islands; similar structures would traditionally be used as food stores or for cooking.

Most low-income Samoans still live in villages in traditional fales, some of which may have a concrete floor, corrugated-iron roof, and latticework walls. When Samoa was hit by two major cyclones in 1990 and 1991—the worst in the islands' recorded history—the fales, with their open sides, stood up better than more modern housing.

SEE ALSO

> Ganvié Stilt Village,
  pages 108–9

> Balinese Kuren,
  pages 154–55

> Kalinga
  Octagonal House,
  pages 156–57

> Aboriginal Shelter,
  pages 164–65

MATERIALS

* Wood for posts
  and columns

* Stone for additional
  protection

* Sugar cane or palm
  leaves for thatch

* Coconut fiber
  for binding

* Palm leaves
  for blinds

* Coral or pebbles
  for flooring

The archipelago of the Samoan islands covers an area of about 1,170 square miles (3,030 sq km) of the central South Pacific.

SAMOA

SUPPORT

The building of a fale tele begins with three main columns supporting a small ridge pole. The columns are initially held up by scaffolding, on which is fastened the lightweight main arc of the roof.

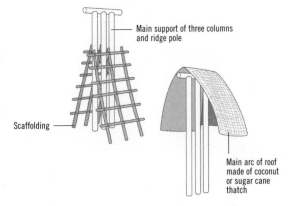

Main support of three columns and ridge pole

Scaffolding

Main arc of roof made of coconut or sugar cane thatch

FRAMEWORK

Next, the two curved ends of the roof are attached, supported by further scaffolding, and the ring of outer posts is put in place. Three different kinds and thicknesses of wood are used in the construction process for posts, rafters, and purlins.

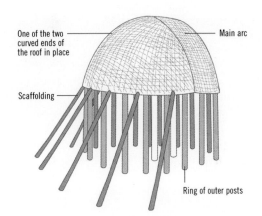

One of the two curved ends of the roof in place

Main arc

Scaffolding

Ring of outer posts

ROOF

The thatched domed roof, which is supported in the center, sits on the outer posts, which steady it and hold it down. The thatch is produced by the women, using sugar cane leaves or palm fronds, overlapped to provide a double coating. The completed building is ringed by stones, which add solidity and keep insects at bay; the size of the stone base is also indicative of status.

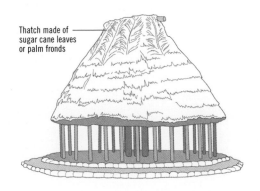

Thatch made of sugar cane leaves or palm fronds

MODERN VERNACULAR ARCHITECTURE

By far the most numerous vernacular buildings of the modern age are the ad hoc constructions of the millions of urban squatters living in city environments across the developing world. In the West, the pressure is on to develop forms and styles of building in tune with the environment, which are energy and water efficient, made of low-carbon and nontoxic materials. Earthships use waste tires filled with rammed earth for walls, and there is a long tradition of buildings made from bottles. Virtually all the material for Ben Law's Woodland House in West Sussex, England, came from the wood itself or from the surrounding area. The interest in reviving old vernacular building skills is illustrated with the cob revival and an African construction scheme to build vaulted roofs without using wood supports.

MODERN VERNACULAR ARCHITECTURE
BRAZILIAN SQUATTER SETTLEMENTS

More than half of the world's population now lives in cities, and this is expected to rise to sixty percent in the next twenty years. Urban growth is most rapid in the developing world, with some cities gaining five million new residents every month. By 2050, the urban population of the developing world will be 5.3 billion, of which sixty-three percent will be in Asia and nearly a quarter in Africa.

One out of every three people in cities of the developing world lives in deprived and unplanned squatter settlements (also referred to as "informal settlements" or "slums"). UN-HABITAT estimates show that in 2005 more than half of the world's "slum" population resided in Asia, followed by sub-Saharan Africa, Latin America, and the Caribbean. According to their report, "State of the World's Cities 2008/2009," "In many parts of the world, these 'invisible,' unplanned parts of cities are growing faster than the more visible, planned parts. In some cities, slum dwellers constitute the majority of the urban population . . . while in others, slums are small pockets of deprivation physically isolated from the rest of the city." The UN measures the degree of deprivation using the following criteria—lack of access to improved water, lack of access to sanitation, nondurable housing, insufficient living area, and security of tenure. Some settlements provide better living conditions than others.

Wherever they are in the world, such settlements share similar characteristics. They arise and grow spontaneously as people pour in from rural areas to try to earn a living in the city and start illegally constructing makeshift shelters, largely built from scrap materials and urban waste. Here, dense populations live in conditions of great poverty without any basic water supplies, sewage drainage, or power supplies. They also live with the constant threat of eviction and the demolition of their homes; a favorite tactic of city authorities is to periodically move in and just flatten them. Despite these problems, many such settlements create strong communities that thrive.

SEE ALSO

> Indian and Filipino Squatter Settlements, pages 174–75

> Ganvié Stilt Village, pages 108–9

MATERIALS

* Scrap lumber for walls and wood stilts
* Corrugated iron for walls and roofs
* Urban waste
* Masonry
* Concrete pillars
* Concrete tiles

Rio de Janeiro is the second-largest city of Brazil and South America. It was the capital of Brazil until 1960, when Brasilia took its place.

RIO DE JANEIRO, BRAZIL

FAVELAS

Among the oldest of squatter settlements and the best-known are the *favelas* of Rio de Janeiro. Today, one-quarter of the city's urban population—about 2.5 million people—live in more than seven hundred favelas, and their number is growing at an annual rate of 7.5 percent. People who live there are known as *favelados*. The vast, chaotic, and changing face of the favelas is made up of thousands of similar fragile shacks on stilts, many of which are built on slopes that have an eighty percent gradient or more. This style of building has a practical purpose, and has evolved to cope with the heavy summer rains of the region. The shacks survive because the water, which washes away many conventionally built structures, simply forks around the stilts, leaving the shacks intact. New favelados first establish their claim by building a small, lightweight, makeshift one-room shack out of scrap materials and urban waste, which sits on a floor of wood boards, supported by stilts firmly anchored in the rock bed. In the next stage, the favelados gradually extend their shack by building covered verandas around it. They then replace all the scavenged materials with more durable ones: wood stilts become concrete pillars, makeshift walls are replaced by masonry, ramshackle roofing by concrete tiles. In a final step, the facade is decorated with ornamentation and painted in a color that reflects the favelados' place of origin.

INDIAN AND FILIPINO SQUATTER SETTLEMENTS

SEE ALSO

> Brazilian Squatter Settlements, pages 172–73

The most famous squatter settlement in the world, mainly as a result of it being used as the location for the Oscar-winning movie *Slumdog Millionaire*, is Dharavi, Asia's largest slum, on the edge of the city of Mumbai in India. Here, an estimated six hundred thousand to one million people are crammed into its 430 acres (174 hectares). This density creates huge practical problems—a single toilet may be shared by several hundred people, and the area is wracked by waterborne diseases—but, says U.S. reporter Bill Dureya, "it is also the engine of its vitality," because more or less every building doubles up as both a residence and a business premises. Economists have estimated that Dharavi's fifteen thousand single-room industries annually generate goods that are worth more than $700 million.

More than nineteen million people live in the rapidly expanding city of Mumbai, and the land on which Dharavi sits is a prime site for redevelopment. But the inhabitants of Dharavi have resisted many attempts by successive governments to move them into modern high-rise buildings with better facilities. Despite the hazards and problems of living in such an environment, they don't like the idea of having to pay extra to live in one place and work in another.

Meanwhile, in the Philippines, a five-year survey has been made of the architecture of informal settlements in Manila, resulting in a book titled *The Evolution of Informality as a Dominant Pattern in Philippine Cities*. The thinking behind it was that the solutions to dealing with Manila's numerous urban problems were more likely to come from observations of the squatter settlements rather than from the thinking of Manila's elite. Photographer Neal Oshima, who documented these communities for the survey, says, "I wonder if these [communities] aren't an optimistic glimmer of the future of the human species on earth."

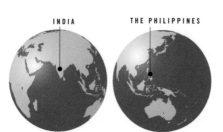

INDIA   THE PHILIPPINES

Manila is ranked as the city with the second-highest population density in the world. Mumbai is ranked seventh highest.

MATERIALS

* Scrap lumber
* Scrap metal roofs
* Urban waste
* Masonry
* Concrete

DHARAVI

The inhabitants of Dharavi live mainly in ramshackle two-story buildings of brick, concrete, and scrap lumber with metal roofs, all parts of which are slightly askew. Bill Dureya says the experience of walking through Dharavi's narrow alleyways is like "navigating a city after a mild earthquake." Yet in 2009, Prince Charles complimented Dharavi for its "underlying, intuitive grammar of design" and the "timeless quality and resilience of vernacular settlements." The residents of Dharavi have created their own world the way they want it to be, largely unfettered by controls and regulations. It has grown informally and constantly changes to suit people's needs, rather than to conform with governmental plans.

MANILA

This is a multistory dwelling in Pineda, Metro Manila, in the Philippines. Photographer Neil Oshima found that most of the squatters in Manila, living in their flimsy dwellings made of discarded materials, were there by choice, despite the poor sanitation, lack of basic facilities, and the risks of flash fires and the threat of violent eviction. He says, 'the architectural solutions were often surprising in their use of materials and space, often redefining the limits of human habitation."

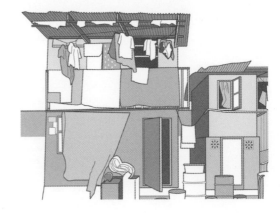

EARTHSHIPS

The earthship is a form of architecture that embraces elements of both the vernacular and technological, and points the way toward a sustainable future. It is a vernacular response to an era of mass production and consumerism. Its creator, Mike Reynolds, calls his work "biotecture"—aimed at creating buildings that are in tune with the natural world. An earthship is a passive solar home made out of recycled and natural materials. It gets its power from the sun and wind, and contains and reuses its own waste water. They are energy efficient and have a low-carbon footprint.

Reynolds, whose work has become internationally recognized through the documentary film *Garbage Warrior,* began developing the Earthship concept in the 1970s. He settled on the rammed-earth tire concept because the basic building block of this new structure as scrap tires are ubiquitous, available locally to all, and this method of converting them into a building material is simple and affordable.

One of the basic principles of Reynold's Earthship Biotecture thinking is that "A sustainable home must make use of indigenous materials, those occurring naturally in the local area. For thousands and thousands of years, housing was built from found materials such as rock, earth, reeds, and logs. Today, there are mountains of by-products of our civilization that are already made and delivered to all areas. These are the natural resources of the modern humanity." The earthship gets most of its power from solar panels and a wind rotor. The roof is designed to capture rainwater and snow melt, which are then channeled through silt catches into cisterns. This water is then used and reused several times—for drinking water, for bathing and washing dishes, and for the flush toilet. Water from sinks and the shower can also be channelled into what Reynolds calls "earthship wetlands"—planters that can be used to grow fresh produce throughout the year.

SEE ALSO

> Indian and Filipino Squatter Settlements, pages 174–75

> Bottle Buildings, pages 178–79

EUROPE

AUSTRALIA AND NEW ZEALAND

Earthships are spreading around the world. They already exist in Europe, Canada, twenty-five U.S. states, the Caribbean, Brazil, and Nicaragua, as well as in Australia and New Zealand.

MATERIALS

* Recycled steel-belt car tires, filled with earth for walls

* Recycled bottles and cans cemented to make interior walls

RECYCLED TIRES

The main building blocks of an earthship are recycled steel-belt rubber car tires, which are rammed full of earth and used as "bricks" to form the walls of the house. These bricks and the resulting bearing walls they form are virtually indestructible and fireproof.

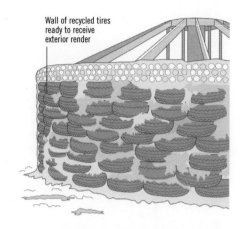

Wall of recycled tires ready to receive exterior render

INTERNAL WALLS

The earthship's internal walls are created using aluminum cans and glass/plastic bottles set in a cement matrix. Both internal and external walls can be shaped to suit the builder's requirements.

Walls made of recycled materials reflect the organic lines of the interior space

COMPLETED EARTHSHIP

An example of a finished earthship. The basic principles of earthship construction can be adapted and customized to suit a wide variety of climates and individual living styles, and have been built around the world. Earthship structures have also been used in disaster relief.

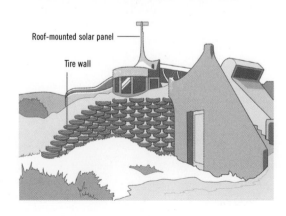

Roof-mounted solar panel

Tire wall

BOTTLE BUILDINGS

The poorest peoples of the world have been building houses out of scrap and garbage as a matter of survival for many years, but in the Western world it was in the 1960s and 1970s that these ideas really began to percolate into modern architectural thought. One of the seminal steps in this regard came in 1963 with the Heineken "World Bottle" (WOBO), an idea inspired by a journey that beer brewer Alfred Heineken made to the Caribbean, where he observed beaches littered with bottles in a society that had a shortage of affordable building materials. On his return, in collaboration with the Dutch architect John Habraken, he devised "the brick that holds beer."

One production run produced one hundred thousand bottles, which were used to build a small shed on Heineken's estate in the Netherlands, but the idea then stalled. Interest was later revived by its inclusion in the seminal book *Garbage Housing* by Martin Pawley, which argued that designing consumer items that, once discarded, could have another use would help address the world's housing crisis.

Bottle houses and structures can now be found in many parts of the world. In the United States, one of the most famous bottle houses is the three-room *L*-shaped Bottle House built in six months in 1905 by seventy-six-year-old saloon owner Tom Kelly in Rhyolite, Nevada, out of fifty-one thousand beer, whiskey, soda, and medicine bottles and adobe. Once a thriving gold-mining center, Rhyolite has now become a ghost town, where Kelly's Bottle House is one of the last buildings standing.

The most impressive bottle structure in the world was built by Buddhist monks from Thailand's Sisaket province, about 370 miles (600 km) northeast of Bangkok. They collected one million bottles, a mixture of green Heineken and brown local Chang beer, to build the Wat Pa Maha Chedi Kaew temple and its associated buildings, including the crematorium. Alfred Heineken would be delighted.

SEE ALSO
> Earthships,
  pages 176–77

NORTH AMERICA   THAILAND

Bottle houses are found in numerous countries of the world. Many in the United States are well-known tourist attractions. Bottle walls are part of many eco-houses.

MATERIALS
* Bottles
* Mortar

BOTTLE WALL

A wall of Heineken World Bottles (WOBO)—"the brick that holds beer." The WOBO came in 13¾-inch (350-mm) and 20-inch (500-mm) versions and was designed to lie horizontally and interlock in a fashion that echoed traditional brick-and-mortar construction.

Horizontally laid bottles cemented to form walls

KELLY'S BOTTLE HOUSE

Kelly's Bottle House in Rhyolite, Nevada, was built in 1905 out of bottles because lumber was scarce at the time. The bottle house was restored and reroofed by Paramount Pictures in 1925 for a movie and was then given to the Beatty Improvement Association for maintenance as an historical site.

Bottles arranged as tiles to form roof covering

BEER-BOTTLE TEMPLE

The Wat Pa Maha Chedi Kaew temple In Thailand must be the world's most unusual bottle building. Here are depicted the main building, a detail of the roof, and a close-up view, which shows how a wall of bottles is constructed.

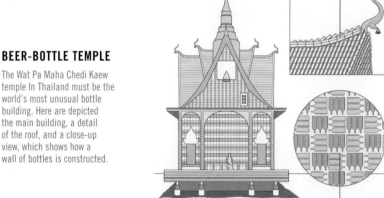

Bottles bonded to form walls, set in square-form pattern

NATURAL BUILDING

In a small country like Britain, where land prices are at a premium and planning laws restrictive, building a modern vernacular building is filled with difficulties, even more so if it's situated in a woodland. Yet that is what permaculturalist and woodland owner Ben Law has achieved with his Woodland House in Prickly Nut Wood, West Sussex. He also captured the imagination of the nation when it was featured on the television program *Grand Designs*.

The form of the house is an A-frame building of four cruck roundwood frames made of sweet chestnut coppice with two roofed verandas and decking on three sides. The whole structure sits on stilts, which, like the traditional cruck frames, are set on foundations of forty-two Yorkshire stone slabs.

The walls of the house are made of a "box" of two larch frames, which are filled with small straw bales. The outside studwork frame is finished with oak and chestnut clapboarding. In between this and the straw is a breathable membrane to provide extra insulation and waterproofing. The roof is made of larch joists with sweet chestnut rafters, overlaid with a waterproof membrane and covered with ten thousand wood shingles. The veranda roofs are covered with a man-made composite material, which is made of bitumen-saturated organic fibers. The inside of the house is open plan, with just three internal doors. The window frames are made of ash, the windows double glazed; the floors are of larch and oak.

The house collects and stores rainwater, pipes waste water out into a series of reed beds for purification, has a compost toilet, and is powered by an array of solar panels and three small wind turbines. Heating is provided by an open fire, and hot water by a back boiler behind a wood-fired range. This beautiful handmade building is virtually entirely constructed from local materials and was built with the help of volunteer labor.

SEE ALSO

> Cruck-Frame Buildings, pages 52–53

MATERIALS

* Cruck roundwood frames of chestnut

* Yorkshire stone slabs

* Larch frames filled with straw bales

* Oak and chestnut clapboarding

* Waterproof membrane

* Wood roof shingles

Britain has a rich historical heritage of vernacular buildings, but land prices and planning laws make building them today difficult.

WEST SUSSEX,
ENGLAND

WOODLAND HOUSE

The completed Woodland House has a strong connection with traditional building that reinforces the building's environmental integrity. This is an example of a modern vernacular design that really does point the way to a more sustainable future. In his book, *The Woodland House,* Ben Law says his house was designed after ten years of observing and getting to know the site he was going to build in and the requirements that the house would need to serve.

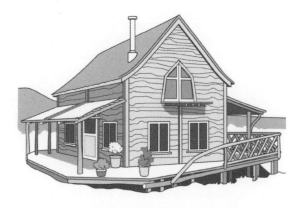

WOOD FRAMEWORK

This interior view of the Woodland House shows the internal wood framework and the underside of the roof with its larch joists and sweet chestnut rafters.

Ridge board supporting rafters

INTERNAL WALLS

These views show the inside of the straw-bale wall and the internal plastering. The bales are first splattered with a coating of thick lime plaster, which fireproofs them and keeps away mice. This is then covered with two layers of a mixture of sharp sand and lime putty, the first of which contains cow and horse hair. The walls are painted with lime wash using natural pigments.

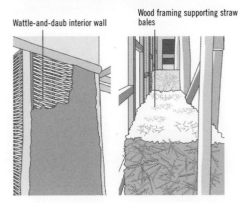

Wattle-and-daub interior wall

Wood framing supporting straw bales

VERNACULAR REVIVALS

The revival of the cob house—a building with thick walls made of an earth-base material of clay, sand, gravel, and subsoil mixed with straw and water—is happening in many parts of the world. This form of house offers an attractive low-cost, low-impact, energy-efficient alternative to conventional homes.

In Devon, England, where cob houses are a traditional vernacular form, the revival began when local builder Kevin McCabe built the first cob residence in the county since seventy years earlier. Another notable project in Britain was Cobtun House in Warwickshire, designed by Associated Architects, which in 2005 won the Royal Institute of British Architects Sustainable Building of the Year Award.

The Oregon-base Cob Cottage Co. started North America's cob revival, which has spread to British Columbia and points farther east since the early 1990s, fueled by rising lumber costs and the sustainable building trend. A Canadian showcase for the revival of cob building is the One United Resource Ecovillage—a 25-acre (10-hectare) sustainable community for forty people on Vancouver Island—due to be completed by 2010.

In West Africa, the Voute Nubienne association is attempting to tackle the problems of house building in the Sahel region by introducing a simplified version of an ancient architectural technique, traditionally used in Sudan and central Asia, that has been adapted to provide protection during the short but heavy rain seasons of sub-Saharan Africa. This technique of earth architecture, known as la Voute Nubienne, or VN, makes it possible to build houses with vaulted roofs without having to use wood shuttering as a support. It uses basic, readily available local materials rather than imported materials and lumber, and can be built using simple, easily learned procedures. The vaults are built of good-quality earth bricks with mortar made of the same earth.

SEE ALSO

> Cob House,
pages 54–55

USA/CANADA   **UK AFRICA**

An estimated two billion people worldwide already live in earth buildings. Environmental pressures are triggering a rise in rammed-earth construction.

MATERIALS

* Cob
* Earth bricks

MODERN DEVON COB HOUSE

This is Keepel Gate, a two-story, four-bedroom thatched cob house built by Devon builder Kevin McCabe. The house was constructed using traditional methods; the only exceptions were that he used a tractor to mix the cob and added sand or shillet (a gravel of crushed shale) to reduce the shrinkage.

PACIFIC NORTHWEST STYLE

This is an example of a Pacific Northwest–style cob house, a form of building that is ideally suited to what is called the "Wet Coast," provided the building has deep overhangs and gutters to protect the earthen walls as well as a high, impervious foundation. Like a ceramic flowerpot, cob absorbs moisture in the air without weakening, and releases it again when it bakes in the sun.

NUBIAN VAULT BUILDING

This lateral cross section of an earthen building employs Nubian vault technology. The wall on the right shows the underlying construction of mud or laterite bricks; on the left, the wall is covered with a final rendering of mud or cement. The roof is waterproofed using locally manufactured plastic sheeting covered with a rendering of enriched mud mortar.

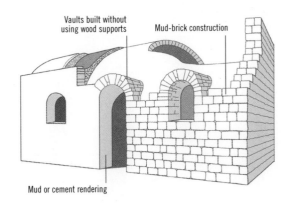

Vaults built without using wood supports   Mud-brick construction

Mud or cement rendering

GLOSSARY

Adobe
An ancient term for "mud brick," dating back some four thousand years to Middle Egypt. In modern English usage, the term also refers to a style of architecture popular in the desert climates of North America.

A-frame
A building constructed with steeply angled sides that meet at the top in the shape of a letter A.

Bargeboard
A decorative board that covers the projecting rafter of the gable end.

Box framing
Type of wood-frame structure where roof trusses are supported on a frame of posts, tie beams, and wall plates.

Clapboarding
The cladding of a building with long thin wood boards that overlap each other, either vertically or horizontally.

Cob
An earth-based building material consisting of subsoil, clay, sand, and gravel, mixed with straw and water and used to build the walls of a house.

Composite
A complex material in which two or more distinct substances are combined to produce structural or functional properties that are not present in any individual component.

Coppice
A grove, copse, or thicket of small trees, especially ones that are regularly pruned to provide a ready supply of poles and firewood.

Corbel
A piece of stone jutting out of a wall to provide additional support. In addition, a technique of building with stone whereby each successive layer is angled slightly inward, thus creating a dome.

Cross brace
A crossbeam used to span an arch, to provide additional stability.

Cruck
An A-shaped wood frame made by splitting a large tree trunk or branch down the middle and fastening the two halves (known as "blades") together at the top with a "collar" or tie beam, so that the curve on each mirrors the other.

Dry-stone
A building method in which structures are built from stones without the use of mortar or clay.

Finial
A sculptured ornament at the tip of a spire or gable.

Fired-earth brick
A molded, rectangular block of clay that is fired in a kiln and used as a building material.

Gable
The triangular wall at the end of a pitched roof.

Gambrel
A two-sided roof with a double slope on each side, the lower part being steeper.

Girder
A beam made of steel, wood, or reinforced concrete, used as a main horizontal support in a building.

Granary
A storehouse for threshed grain.

Hip
A type of roof with no gables, where all sides of the roof form a gentle slope to the walls.

Joist
Parallel planks or beams that hold up the planks of a floor or the laths of a ceiling.

Lath
A thin strip of wood, nailed in rows to a supporting frame, that acts as a substructure for shingles, slates, or tiles.

Load-bearing
Structural elements, typically walls, that function as support for roofs and floors.

Masonry
Construction using stone, brick, or concrete.

Mortar
A masonry product composed of cement and sand. When water is mixed with mortar, its binding element, the cement, is activated.

Mortise and tenon
A method of joining two pieces of wood whereby a projection (tenon) on the end of one piece of wood fits into a corresponding slot (mortise) on the other.

Palisade
A strong fence made of stakes or pales that forms a defensive barrier or fortification.

Piling
A column of wood, steel, or concrete that is driven into the ground to provide support for a structure.

Planking
A long flat piece of lumber that is thicker than a board; laying, covering, or furnishing with planks.

Purlin
One of several horizontal wood components supporting the rafters of a roof.

Rafter
A sloping beam that supports a pitched roof.

Rammed earth
A method of construction whereby walls are built by compacting an earth mixture into a framework of slats, called a "form," to create an earth brick.

Render
To cover a masonry surface with a first coat of plaster.

Ridge beam/pole
The highest horizontal beam at the ridge of a roof to which the rafters are attached; the horizontal pole at the top of a tent.

Ring beam
A beam that runs around the base of a dome to prevent it from spreading.

Rubble
Rough stone, broken brick, and masonry, typically used for infill and foundations.

Shingle
A thin oblong piece of material, usually wood or slate, that is laid in overlapping rows to cover the roof or the sides of a building.

Thatch
Plant stalks or foliage used for covering roofs, including straw, reeds, palm fronds, heather, and ferns, usually tied down with rope or braided straw.

Tongue and groove
A joint made by a tongue on one edge of a board fitting into a corresponding groove on another.

Truss
A rigid structural framework of wood that provides support for purlins.

Turf
A section of grass-covered earth, cut out and used as a building material for covering walls and roofs from ancient times. It provides insulation and is fireproof.

Wattle and daub
A building material consisting of interwoven rods, twigs, or laths, plastered with mud or clay; a form of wall construction or material used as infill between the members of a wood-frame wall.

RESOURCES

FURTHER READING

General
Atlas of Vernacular Architecture of the World,
Marcel Vellinga, Paul Oliver, Alexander Bridge
(Routledge, 2007)

Built By Hand: Vernacular Buildings Around the World,
Bill and Athena Steen, Eiko Komatsu; photos by Yoshio
Komatsu (Gibbs Smith, 2003)

Dwellings, Paul Oliver (Phaidon 2003)

Earth Architecture, Ronald Rael
(Princeton Architectural Press, 2008)

The Encyclopaedia of Vernacular Architecture,
Editor Paul Oliver (Cambridge University Press, 1998)

Home Work: Handbuilt Shelter, Lloyd Kahn
(Shelter Publications, 2004)

Shelter, Editor Lloyd Kahn (Shelter Publications, 1973)

Traditional Buildings, Allen G. Noble (I.B. Tauris, 2007)

Vernacular Architecture in the Twenty-First Century
Lindsay Asquith, Marcel Vellinga (Taylor & Francis,
2006)

Europe and Eurasia
Architecture In Wood: A World History,
Will Pryce (Thames & Hudson, 2005)

The Changing World: The Lapps, Arthur Spence
(David & Charles, 1978)

Discovering Timber-Framed Buildings,
Richard Harris (Shire Publications, 1993)

The Dutch Windmill, Frederick Stokhuyzen
(C.A.J. van Dishoeck-Bussum-Holland, 1962)

"House Traditions in the Outer Hebrides: The Black
House and the Beehive Hut," Werner Kissling in *Man*,
(Vol. 44, Nov–Dec. 1944, pp. 134–140 / Royal
Anthropological Society of Great Britain)

Russian Folk Art, Alison Hilton
(Indiana University Press, 1995)

*The Wooden Churches of Eastern Europe:
An Introductory Survey*, David Buxton
(Cambridge University Press, 1981)

The Mediterranean and Middle East
"Climatic responsive architecture in hot and dry
regions of Iran," A. A'zami, S.H. Yasrebi, A. Salehipoor
(International Conference "Passive and Low Energy
Cooling for the Built Environment," May 2005,
Santorini, Greece)

La Tente Noire, C. G. Feilberg
(Gyldendalske Boghandel Nordisk Forlag, 1944)

"Malta Troglodytica; Ghar il-Kbir," A. Luttrell in
Heritage, (Vol. 2, 1979, pp. 461–4)

Asia
China's Old Dwellings, Ronald G. Knapp
(University of Hawaii Press, 2000)

*Chinese Earth-Sheltered Dwellings: Indigenous
Lessons for Modern Urban Design*, Gideon S. Golany
(University of Hawaii Press, 1992)

The Complete Yurt Handbook, Paul King
(Eco-Logic Books / Worldly Goods, 2001)

Japanese Folkhouses, Norman F. Carver, Jr.
(Documan Press Ltd., 1984)

Japan's Folk Architecture, Chuji Kawashima
(Kodansha International, 1986)

Steps to Water: The Ancient Stepwells of India,
Morna Livingston (Princeton Architectural Press, 2002)

*What is Japanese Architecture?: A Survey of Traditional
Japanese Architecture*, Kazuo Nishi, Kazuo Hozumi,
H. Mack Horton (Kodansha International, 1996)

Sub-Saharan Africa
After Kinship, Janet Carsten
(Cambridge University Press, 2004)

The Anatomy of Architecture, Suzanne Preston Blier
(University of Chicago Press, 1994)

*From Cameroon to Paris: Mousgoum In and
Out of Africa*, Steven Nelson (University of Chicago
Press, 2007)

"Indlu: the domed dwelling of the Zulu,"
Barrie E. Biermann in *Shelter in Africa*,
Editor Paul Oliver (Barrie & Jenkins, 1971)

"Lacustrine Villages in South Benin as Refuges from the Slave Trade," Eliseé Soumonni in *Fighting the Slave Trade*, Editor Sylviane A. Diouf (James Currey Publishers, 2003)

"The Resurrection of the House amongst the Zafimaniry," Maurice Bloch in *Material Culture: Critical Concepts in the Social Sciences*, Victor Buchli (Taylor & Francis, 2004)

North America
Ancient Architecture of the Southwest, William N. Morgan (University of Texas Press, 1994)

Classic Cracker: Florida's Wood-Frame Vernacular Architecture, Ronald W. Haase (Pineapple Press, 1992)

The Indian Tipi: Its History, Construction, and Use, Reginald Laubin (University of Oklahoma Press, 2001)

Kentucky Folk Architecture, William Lynwood Montell, Michael Lynn Morse (University of Kentucky Press, 1995)

Native American Architecture, Peter Nabokov, Robert Easton (Oxford University Press, 1989)

Tipi: Home of the Nomadic Buffalo Hunters, Paul Goble, Rodney Frey (World Wisdom Books, 2007)

Latin America
Empire of the Senses: The Sensual Culture Reader, David Howes (Berg Publishers, 2005)

Australasia and Oceania
Artistic Heritage in a Changing Pacific, Editors Philip J. C. Dark, Roger G. Rose (University of Hawaii Press, 1993)

The Continuum Encyclopedia of Native Art: Worldview, Symbolism, and Culture in Africa, Oceania, and North America, Hope B. Werness (Continuum International Publishing Group, 2000)

Gunyah, Goondie & Wurley, Paul Memmott (University of Queensland Press, 2007)

Introduction to Balinese Architecture, Julian Davison (Periplus Editions, 1993)

The Korowai of Irian Jaya: Their Language in Its Cultural Context, Gerrit J. van Enk, Lourens de Vries (Oxford University Press, 1997)

Treehouses, Paul Henderson, Adam Mornement (Frances Lincoln, 2005)

Modern Vernacular Architecture
The Woodland House, Ben Law (2nd edition. Permanent Publications, 2009)

WEB SITES
20 Amazingly Unique Architectural Designs of Houses from Around the World
http://tinyurl.com/lsy5ze

Earth Architecture
www.eartharchitecture.org

Green Home Building
www.greenhomebuilding.com

The International Vernacular Architecture Unit
www.brookes.ac.uk/schools/be/oisd/act/ivau/index.htm

Vernacular Architecture Forum
www.vernaculararchitectureforum.org

Vernacular Designs
www.greatbuildings.com/architects/Vernacular.html

This book has drawn on the work of the following authors in *The Encyclopedia of Vernacular Architecture*: Joseph L. Aranha, Dierdrie Brown, Tara Michele Cahn, Miles Danby, Philip Drew, Patrick Dujarric, Michael W. Earls, Andus Emge, Rosario Encarnacion-Tan, Fauzia Farneti, Lorenzo Fonseca, Gulliermo Vasquez De Velasco De La Fuente, Anders Grum, Ingebjørg Hage, Lynne Hancock, John Raymond Harrison, Brigitta Hauser-Schaublin, Molly Lee, David Lung, Helen Mulligan, William A. Noble, Tohru Ogawa, Paul Oliver, Anthony Quiney, Gregory A. Reinhardt, Alberto Saldarriaga Roa, Susan Roaf, David G. Saile, Reimar Schefold, Anastasie Sulistyawati, Colin Taylor, William P. Thompson, Fernando Varanda, John Michael Vlach, Anthony G. Vogt, James Walton, James P. Warfield, Stephen White.

INDEX

ACKNOWLEDGMENTS

AUTHOR ACKNOWLEDGMENTS

Making a book like this is the product of many minds and hands, and the author would like to thank the following: consultant Anthony Reid for bringing his expert knowledge and experience to bear on a book that has been enriched by his valuable contributions; illustrator Coral Mula for handling a complex task with great skill, her work adding immeasurably to the value of this volume; Caroline Earle and Michael Whitehead, for handling the book's production in such a scrupulous, professional, and positive manner; to Jason Hook and Sophie Collins for giving me the opportunity to explore this fascinating subject; and Sarah Clowes for making the valuable introductions that started me off on this interesting journey.

PICTURE CREDITS

The publisher would like to thank the following individuals and organizations for their kind permission to reproduce the images in this book. Every effort has been made to acknowledge the pictures, however, we apologize if there are any unintentional omissions.

Alamy/Hemis: 11b; Danita Delimont: 12; China Images: 25; GeoffMarshall: 32b; Images of Africa Photobank: 33c; Stuart Forster India: 35b.

© **Art in All of Us:** /Anthony Asael: 26

Corbis: /Anders Ryman: 32t; Albrecht G. Schaefer: 34t; Bo Zaunders: 34b; Nik Wheeler: 36t; Rungroj/epa: 37, 38.

Getty Images: /Peter Adams: front cover.

Fotolia: /Richard Majlinder: 9b; Anatoly Repin: 10t; jpskenn: 11t; Jeff Gynane: 13t; rolafoto: 14b; Michael Shake: 17t; Paco Ayala: 20b; Jeremy Richards: 21t; PixAchi: 22c; Jan Reinke: 27c; Bernardo Ertl: 28t; travellingtwo: 33b; Fiorelino: 35t; MJPHOTO: 138–39.

iStockphoto: 7, 9t; Branko Habjan: 10b; Phil Augustavo: 13b; Margo van Leeuwen: 15; Ariadne Van Zandbergen: 16t; Rich Woodfin: 17b; 20t; Ints Tomsons: 21b; Stephen Finn: 22t; Mustafa Can: 24b; Ines Gesell: 27t; 27b; Cliff Parnell: 31t; Alberto L. Pomares G.: 39t; Hilary Fox: 39b; Joseph Bergevin: 44; Nitin Sanil: 45r; Bruno Buongiorno: 45l; Sean Randall: 68–69; 84–85; Alan Tobey: 102–3; Jason Doucette: 120–21; MJPHOTO: 170–71.

Jupiter Images: 2, 8, 11c, 14t, 14c, 16b, 16c, 18l, 18tr, 19, 22b, 23, 24t, 28b, 29, 30b, 33tl, 33tr, 36b, 40t, 40b, 41, 43, 46–47, 152–53.

Photolibrary: 30t.

© **José V. Resino:** 31b.